Garrett Theological Studies

NUMBER ONE

Dennis Groh
Samuel Laeuchli
Ernest Saunders
John Schreiber
Jerry Stewardson

Edited by
Samuel Laeuchli ∧

With a Preface by
Giovanni Becatti

MITHRAISM
IN
OSTIA

Mystery Religion and Christianity
in the Ancient Port of Rome

NORTHWESTERN UNIVERSITY PRESS

Contents

References

Be-Mi   BECATTI, G. *Scavi di Ostia*. II. *I Mitrei*. Rome, 1954.

Cu-Mi   CUMONT, FRANZ. *The Mysteries of Mithra*. Translated from the second revised edition by T. J. McCormack. New York, 1956.

Cu-Or   CUMONT, FRANZ. *The Oriental Religions in Roman Paganism*. New York, 1956.

Me   MEIGGS, R. *Roman Ostia*. Oxford, 1960.

Sq   SQUARCIAPINO, M. F. *I Culti Orientali ad Ostia*. Leiden, 1962.

To   CALZA, G.; BECATTI, G.; GISMONDI, I.; DE ANGELIS D'OSSAT, G.; and BLOCH, H. *Scavi di Ostia*. I. *Topografia Generale*. Rome, 1954.

Ve-Corp   VERMASEREN, M. J. *Corpus Inscriptionum et Monumentorum Religionis Mithraicae*, Vols. I and II. The Hague, 1956, 1960.

Ve-Mi   VERMASEREN, M. J. *Mithras, The Secret God.* Translated from the 1960 Paris work by T. and V. Megaw. New York, 1963.

Ve-Prisc   VERMASEREN, M. J., and VAN ESSEN, C. C. *The Excavations in the Mithraeum of Santa Prisca in Rome*. Leiden, 1965.

Preface

WITH GREAT ADMIRATION I have watched this select group of American scholars come to Ostia to study the various aspects of Mithraism displayed in this ancient city. It made me remember with pleasure and satisfaction the period of my life in which this fascinating subject was the center of my work. Mithraism is certainly one of the most significant religious phenomena of the imperial period and therefore one of the most important components of the climate in which the Christian church matured.

The result of my American colleagues' sojourn at Ostia is presented in this collection of intimately and accurately documented articles. These scholars of the New World were indeed able to penetrate the complex topographical picture of Ostia with all the urban, archaeological, and environmental factors involved in such research. They relived the atmosphere of the Mithraea, perceiving and pinpointing the most typical and urgent problems of Mithraism.

The research team engaged in mutual discussions and subdivided the tasks so that the various chapters offer a series of interesting perspectives. The characteristic structure of the Mithraea is clearly defined by Dennis Groh. Their distribution in the various districts, and their relation to granaries and baths, are evaluated with astute observations by John Schreiber. He includes a useful synoptic chart. As Mr. Schreiber says, however, his conclusions in regard to the rise and expansion of Mithraism (spreading from the center and the south-central part of the city around the temenos of the Magna Mater first west and northwest and then southeast and east) are naturally based on an analysis of excavations up to this time, and may have to be modified by new discoveries toward the Tiber and also toward the sea. We shall have to wait and see if such new excavations bring us surprises.

Among the most important Mithraic discoveries during the past several years outside Ostia is the Mithraeum of Marino, which is also the most picturesque of all. (The Mithraeum of Marino is included in the research.) Since this discovery is taken for granted in this book and since it is not yet known in wider circles, I take the liberty of informing the reader of this remarkable discovery. For centuries it was customary for vintners of Marino to excavate their basements, which lay on volcanic tufa, in order to store their celebrated wine. When one such cave was enlarged and a wall was torn down, a vintner discovered, to his great surprise, another cave, all hewn out and ready for use. It was whitewashed and painted, with Mithraic *podia* constructed as if to carry the wine casks along the inner wall. Such a singular "Dionysiac" transformation on the site of a Mithraeum is one of those many surprising aspects of our old classical world, where the ancient and the new coexist and unite in a millennial picture—in this case without causing any harm to the Mithraeum. The most dazzling aspect of this sanctuary was a series of pictures, with the bull in the middle and a precious sequence of scenes on the Mithraic myth to the right and left of the *tauroctonos*. We have photographed this spectacular sequence and reproduced it in color in the *Encyclopedia dell' Arte Antica*. From the sequences on the right side of the picture, Jerry Stewardson and

Ernest Saunders justifiably conclude that, contrary to the sequences of Mithraic mythology established by Franz Cumont, the slaughter of the bull must have preceded rather than followed the kneeling of the sun in front of Mithra and the agreement between the two protagonists.

Samuel Laeuchli demonstrates that the language of the Mithraic symbols was not specifically "Mithraic." I wish to enforce this case. The same symbol may indeed acquire a significant difference in a different context. The same *krater* that in the Mithraea is able to refer to the blood of the bull for the regenerative purification of the initiated could become, as in the mosaics of the *Caupone*, a symbol of the water which was mixed with the wine, while in a Christian context it became a symbol of the water of eternal salvation. This symbolization of Mithraism has been brilliantly investigated in its various aspects in Samuel Laeuchli's article. He may be going too far in believing that he is able to identify and distinguish the animus of the military, the slave, and the merchant during the Mithraic ritual; but he indeed appropriately focuses the attention upon the social factors in Mithraism, the social experience of the initiate, and the transfer of the culture to the intimacy of the sanctuaries and houses. In the final article he analyzes this Mithraic phenomenon as the great foe to Christianity in its related and reciprocal influences.

Ostia offers dramatic evidence in one point where Mithraism was certainly at a disadvantage in its struggle with the Christian church, and this is in its exclusion of women from the Mithraic cult. I am thinking of the two first-century temples at Ostia dedicated to the Bona Dea and reserved for women. In this cult, secret and mysterious like Mithraism, women found a religious experience analogous to that of Mithra. In the case of the Mithraeum of Felicissimus, the two temples appear side by side, thereby demonstrating the separation into male and female cults, a separation which the Christian church did not follow to this degree.

As an "Ostiense" I am pleased indeed that this book makes a valid contribution to the knowledge of the religious and social aspects of Ostia. It was a great pleasure to have been able to express in these few lines my appreciation for the scholarly work by my friends from Evanston, and I express my deep joy in the academic and human friendships offered by such a project.

GIOVANNI BECATTI

Ostia Antica
September 8, 1966

Mithraism in Ostia

The Project

A NUMBER OF CONSIDERATIONS led to the "Ostia Project," a concentrated study of the archaeological remains of the ancient port of Rome for five weeks in the summer of 1965 by a team of professors and graduate students from Garrett Theological Seminary. A great deal of work is being done in Biblical archaeology, not merely by the archaeologists themselves but by Old Testament scholars who make use of and interpret the excavations. When it comes to scholarship in New Testament, church history, and historical theology, there is much greater reluctance to enter the interpretative task in regard to imperial archaeology and art. This is partly due to the fact that the historian or Biblical scholar is not competent in this field; yet, the vast archaeological discoveries of the past decades present major challenges to Christian history, from the new synagogue at Sardis to the Roman cemeterial basilicas excavated by Friedrich Deichmann. Such a meeting ground of imperial archaeology and historical studies contains a two-way stream; the Christian historian enters the ancient world by an avenue that is otherwise inaccessible, but he also brings along a knowledge of texts which enables him to see connections often missed by archaeologists. While archaeological discoveries contribute directly to Christian studies, they also may profit from conclusions which scholars in related fields can draw. The task of the Ostia project was to learn from one specific problem in archaeological research. By immersing itself in the specific issue of Roman Mithraism, the research team came to its own conclusions.

There is a second value in such archaeological research and interpretation. As we study the amazingly well-preserved port of ancient Rome, we do not merely read texts but we have a concrete, visual access, at least to the contours, the layout, and the remains of this city. It is one thing to read an early Christian text, and it is another to walk over the alleys and squares in which such a text was made possible. Not that we ever have a direct access—it is the modern scholar who walks over what has been excavated, and most of the Ostian marble is now structured into the Cathedral of Pisa; nevertheless, we are given an entry into the atmosphere and framework of ancient life which is an exceedingly valuable complement to textual research.

The value of such a meeting ground between historical-Christian and archaeological-cultural studies can be shown in the over-all impact which Ostia makes even without our considerations of Mithraism. Here is a city of the first three hundred years of Christianity (see Plate 1); its history, its social, political, and economic character, and its religious movements are written in its brick and marble. We find the shift from *domus* to *insula*, from private house to apartment house, gradually developing during the Trajanic, Hadrianic, and Antonine periods. We observe the growth of a working-class and freedmen society during the second century. We perceive the decline of prosperity until finally Ostia doomed itself by siding with the defeated Maxentius against Constantine. The port had begun to silt up long before this. The examination of the development of Christianity lacks the essential elements if the imperial society, the apartment-house world, and the economic strata within the Roman melting pot are not considered.

PLATE I   An Ostian Insula and Street

There is a third dimension which led to the Ostia Project. The most spectacular discoveries at Ostia itself were those many Mithra sanctuaries (*Mithraea*) described in the volume of the *Scavi di Ostia* by Giovanni Becatti. While half a century ago Mithraism was seen as a vital parallel to rising Christianity, relatively few scholars have taken seriously any of the new Mithraic discoveries, not merely at Ostia but at Santa Prisca in Rome, at Marino, in England, and elsewhere. The necessity to reopen the Mithra problem in the whole scope of early Christian studies becomes obvious to anyone examining the new corpus of Mithraic material by Vermaseren. To study the Mithraea of Ostia was the specific task of this project.

We must mention a fourth consideration, which we hope will be applied in future projects. The time has passed in which one man could master the entirety of a field, even to a limited degree. Academic team research is the only alternative to that impasse between minute specific scholarship and incompetent generalization. Team research in early Christian studies should include not only Biblical scholars and historians with different specialties but also classicists, archaeologists, and specialists in artistic, economic, and social histories. The Ostia research fulfilled this demand in part by consulting the specialists in the excavations and by inviting scholars with different interests to participate. We would hope that this type of team research could be developed on a considerably broader base.

Such were some of the ideas behind the Ostia Project. Before the project, there were careful preparations by graduate students. At Ostia itself, the task was divided. (Plate 2.) Professor Ernest Saunders and Jerry Stewardson studied the symbolism of Mithraic liturgy and worship; Professor Edward Blair and Dennis Groh analyzed the Mithraea themselves; John Schreiber and I examined the Mithraea in relation to the neighborhoods of Ostia; and Professor Albert Sundberg served as consultant observer. The topics overlapped, of course, and the results were always exchanged. In the months following the return, a seminar evaluated the work, and the articles in this book are the results of this evaluation. They present primarily the Mithraic problem itself, a first step toward a new debate on Christianity and Mithraism that is overdue in early Christian studies. As a beginning and an example

6

PLATE 2   The Members of the Ostia Project

of the kind of interpretative venture we hope to stimulate, a final
essay on "Christ and Mithra" has been included.

Although at first sight this book seems to be concerned primarily
with Mithraism, it is, if seen from the perspective of early Christian work,
of direct relevance to this Christian work itself. Here is the church's
time-bound and local habitation; here are the environment, the religious
competitor, the parallel symbolism. This book therefore invites the reader to
grasp Christianity not in any docetic fashion, as if texts spoke in timeless
aeons, but to visualize it in its historical concreteness. In the brickstamps and
inscriptions of Ostia's *insulae*, crowded with a mixed Mediterranean
population, we have not only the history of Rome and Mithra but also
the historical background behind early Christianity.

We are grateful to Dwight Loder and Orville McKay, who made this
project possible, and to our librarian, John Batsel, for his support in this work.
We acknowledge our real appreciation to the directors and staff of the
Scavi di Ostia for their full cooperation; and we thank Professor
Giovanni Becatti for giving us an opportunity to discuss our
research one afternoon in his home.

Samuel Laeuchli

The Ostian Mithraeum

DENNIS GROH

SPREAD THROUGHOUT THE CITY OF OSTIA are her
fourteen best-preserved sanctuaries of the pagan god Mithra. The sanctuaries,
or *Mithraea*, studied were the Animals, Seven Doors, Planta Pedis, House
of Diana, Painted Walls, Seven Spheres, Imperial Palace, Lucretius Menander,
Baths of Mithra, Fructosus, Felicissimus, Sabazeo, Porta Romana, and the
Serpents (listed in their chronological order.)[1] To introduce the study of
Ostian Mithraism, this paper will first lay out the basic elements of a
Mithraeum at Ostia; in a second part, significant variations from the "typical"
Mithraeum will be described. Unless otherwise specified, descriptions
are based on structures and monuments *in situ*.

1. The Sacello of the Three Naves is not considered to be a Mithraeum and is
therefore not included in this list. However, findings from the Three Naves and from
three major Mithraea at Rome (San Clemente, Santa Prisca, and the Baths of Caracalla)
will be used to clarify problems relating to the Mithraea of Ostia.

9

A Typical Mithraeum

An Ostian Mithraeum consists essentially of a rectangular room in
which members of the cult worshiped. The sole exception to this pattern is
the somewhat square room of the Fructosus, whose atypical shape can be
attributed to the fact that the structure was initially intended to be a collegiate,
or guild, temple.[2] It is to this rectangular room that we shall apply the
term "Mithraeum"; we shall call any additional rooms "adjacent rooms."[3]

The Mithraea at Ostia vary considerably in size, ranging from the large
Imperial Palace ($56' \times 18'$) and the Baths of Mithra ($55' \times 13'$) to the small
Lucretius Menander ($26' \times 14'$) and the Fructosus ($15\frac{1}{2}' \times 19'$).[4] However,
nine of the Mithraea are forty-one feet in length, or less; the majority of
these are between thirty and forty feet in length. Thus the average Ostian
Mithraeum is thirty to forty feet long and thirteen to eighteen feet wide.

All of the Mithraea are entered from the rear.[5] Although several
have more than one entrance, the majority have only the single entrance at
the rear. This suggests that the rear was the preferred place of entering
and was probably the only one used by the worshipers.

In seven Mithraea the entrances are located in the rear wall and open
directly into the aisle of the room. In five sanctuaries the entrances are located
in the rear section of the right wall, and in two others they are located in
the rear of the left wall. But in all of them the worshiper would have
been facing the front wall as he started down the central aisle.

Access to this rear entrance is sometimes gained by means of a hallway or

2. Fructosus was converted to a Mithraeum after construction on the temple had
begun but before it was completed.

3. Baths of Mithra, Felicissimus, and Planta Pedis have rooms adjacent to the
main sanctuary.

4. Measurements given throughout this paper are approximations based on plans
in *Be-Mi* and the text in *Ve-Corp* and on our own calculations. For exact measurements
see *Be-Mi*.

5. "Rear" in this paper refers to the narrow end of the main room opposite the
worship center (which end is referred to as the "front"). "Left" or "right" means left
or right as one faces the worship center at the front wall.

foyer leading to the inner sanctuary door (as in the Animals, Lucretius Menander, Fructosus, Serpents, Imperial Palace, and Sabazeo), or access is gained through an adjacent room (as in Felicissimus); but none of the entrances is located directly on (or near) a main street or square.

The rear door which opens into the Mithraeum reveals a single central aisle which runs the length of the room to the worship center at the front. The central aisles of seven Mithraea contain mosaics, which vary in subject matter and quality of workmanship. Some of the aisles have extremely interesting mosaics. For example, the aisle of the Seven Spheres is divided into seven sections by half-circles placed at intervals along the floor. The Animals has depictions of a standing male figure (holding a *falx* and shovel), a raven, a scorpion, a serpent, and a bull's head with a sacrificial knife next to it. But the most interesting and valuable mosaics are found in the Felicissimus, where the seven grades of Mithraic initiation are symbolically depicted (see Plate 3).[6]

A feature which will receive further treatment below is that in nine Ostian Mithraea small basins are set into the floor of the aisle at various places. In Porta Romana, House of Diana, Imperial Palace, and Felicissimus[7] the basins are located just inside the rear entrance. In Seven Spheres there is a basin at the right rear side of the central aisle. Painted Walls and Seven Doors have one in the center-front area, and Sabazeo has one halfway down the aisle and slightly left of center. There is also a small *nymphaeum* at the doorway leading to the entry corridor of the Animals.

Two *podia* running parallel to the central aisle are built into each side of the Mithraeum. These are usually constructed of brick and mortar (and are sometimes decorated at the aisle edges with mosaics, as in Seven Spheres and Seven Doors) and extend from the aisle to the wall on each side (see Plate 4). The podia often slope from the aisle toward the wall to allow the worshiper to recline comfortably in accordance with the common

6. Descriptions of the mosaics of the Seven Spheres, Animals, and Felicissimus can be found in *Ve-Corp*, I, Inscr. 240; p. 134, Inscr. 279; and pp. 140-41, Inscr. 299, respectively.

7. This assumes that what is called a "stylized tree" (*Ve-Corp*, I, Inscr. 299) is a basin. We fail to see why a representation of a tree should be hollowed in the center.

PLATE 3   The Mithraeum of Felicissimus

Roman practice. Because of the podia, most of the floor space of a Mithraeum is taken up, thereby decreasing further the size of the room.

The importance of such podia to a Mithraeum is attested by the fact that twelve sanctuaries have podia *in situ*, and M. J. Vermaseren claims to have found remains of them in a thirteenth.[8] Although the Planta Pedis (the fourteenth Mithraeum) has only small benches, on which the worshipers would have had to sit upright, there is no reason to suppose that a sacred meal could not have been held there.[9]

While podia in some Mithraea extend the length of the room (i.e., to the front wall on either side of the aisle), the right podium in several Mithraea stops short of the front wall, leaving an unoccupied space in the right front corner (in Painted Walls, Serpents, Lucretius Menander, Imperial Palace, Porta Romana, and Baths of Mithra).

Podia in eight of the Mithraea[10] have small niches (usually square) at floor level. These are often located opposite each other (one on a side) and halfway down the aisle.

At the front of each Mithraeum is a worship center, which usually consists of a large altar, a *bema*, and a niche in which the familiar *tauroctonos* figure always appeared.

Altars of differing types are located at the head of the aisle in Baths of Mithra, Planta Pedis (Plate 5), Seven Doors, Lucretius Menander, and Serpents.[11] Sometimes the altar is built directly into the lower steps of the bema, as in the Imperial Palace and Painted Walls. One of the common

8. In the Fructosus (*Ve-Corp*, I, Inscr. 226).

9. In the museum of Ostia there is a banquet scene in which two people are sitting upright on a bench (catalogue number 10). It is also possible either that the two adjacent rooms at Planta Pedis were used for the cult meal or that the facilities of another Mithraeum were employed.

10. The Serpents is included in these eight Mithraea. Although its podia were too damaged for any niches to be identified, Vermaseren (*Ve-Corp*, I, Inscr. 294) reported finding niches in both podia. The eight with niches are Serpents, Lucretius Menander, Planta Pedis, Sabazeo, Seven Doors, Porta Romana (one in the right podium; the other podium too damaged to tell), Seven Spheres, and Painted Walls (four niches).

11. Although there is no altar at Fructosus, there are what appear to be supports for a *mensa*, which probably replaced the altar. In only four Mithraea was there no altar *in situ*.

PLATE 4 The Mithraeum of the Seven Spheres

PLATE 5   The Mithraeum of the Planta Pedis

types is the square altar of brick-and-mortar construction which was originally faced with marble or fresco. The I-shaped altar of solid rock also seems to have been popular.

In addition to the large central altars, smaller ones are found at various places in five Mithraea. The importance of those in Seven Spheres, Baths of Mithra, and Serpents needs to be stressed. The Seven Spheres had two small altars, cupped on top, which were built into the back corners of the podia. The Baths of Mithra has a similar arrangement on the front corners of the podia. On this basis we assume that the single cupped altar found in the Serpents stood with a mate on a podium corner. The fact that flat places are found on the corners of both podia reinforces this assumption.

Directly behind the altar, and set against the front wall, is a stepped bema. The bema may be a large structure with as many as five stages (as in the Imperial Palace) or a smaller one with as few as two stages (as in the Serpents). Seven of the fourteen Mithraea have bemas.[12] The House of Diana has an *aedicula* instead of a bema.[13] The Seven Doors has no bema because such a structure would cover up a mosaic; therefore, the tauroctonos relief was affixed directly to the front wall. The Fructosus, probably because of its small size ($15\frac{1}{2}' \times 19'$), has a niche carved roughly out of the wall. The Baths of Mithra uses Kriton's large statue of Mithra slaying the bull instead of a bema.[14]

The bema is usually of the same width as the aisle. It rises to an elevated niche in which is found the representation of Mithra slaying the bull. Sometimes the niche is set into the front wall; sometimes it is formed by the structure of the bema itself.[15] It is almost certain that every Mithraeum

12. This number includes Sabazeo, which has only three steps remaining at the front end since the entire structure is broken down to a height of about two feet.

13. This type of aedicula, rounded at the top, has been termed a "pseudo-aedicula" by G. K. Boyce, who says it is a development out of the wall niche in imperial times (G. K. Boyce, *Corpus of the Lararia of Pompeii* [*Memoirs of the American Academy in Rome*, Vol. XIV], p. 13).

14. See *Ve-Corp*, I, Fig. 69, for a picture of this excellent statue.

15. It is difficult to be specific about the exact arrangement, since the front walls of six Mithraea are broken away below the niche (Lucretius Menander, Serpents, Sabazeo, Porta Romana, Imperial Palace, and Animals).

had the tauroctonos figure as its central object or focus of worship.[16]

Thus far we have described a "typical" Ostian Mithraeum. There must have been a considerable unity of cultic myth and liturgy by which the community was defined.[17] However, it must also be emphasized that each of the Mithraea has its own personality and differs in specific details from all others. Initially it was thought that the diversity might be due to a structural development which could have evolved over the one hundred fifty years of Mithraeum-building (that is, from the Animals, *ca.* 160 A.D., to the Serpents, *ca.* 250–300 A.D.). But no such development could be established. Next it was thought that this diversity might seem greater than it actually was because the whole spectrum was being studied. But when data gathered from Mithraea built about the same time were juxtaposed and compared,[18] no pattern which could reduce or systematize the diversity among the Mithraea emerged.

Other factors were employed to explain the individuality of each sanctuary. All Ostian Mithraea were constructed in previously existing buildings; therefore, they had to be adapted (within certain limits) to the kinds of space available. Economic inequalities among Mithraic congregations accounted for further diversity.[19] Finally, individual tastes probably caused many of the differences in structures and furnishings.

16. *Cu-Mi*, p. 166.

17. Hans Jonas (*The Gnostic Religion*, 2d rev. ed. [Boston: Beacon, 1958], p. 42) has postulated a similar unity of "basic myth" amidst the diversity of Gnosticism. The standardized tauroctonos relief contributed to this unity in Mithraism (*Cu-Mi*, p. 24).

18. For example, data gathered from the Seven Doors (160–70 A.D.), Animals (*ca.* 160 A.D.), and Planta Pedis (176–80 A.D.) were examined for similarity and difference. Then data gathered from Fructosus (*ca.* 250 A.D.) and Serpents (250–300 A.D.) were likewise examined. Finally, data from earlier groupings of Mithraea were compared with those from later ones.

19. The congregation which built the Sabazeo, with its rude and poorly executed mosaic inscription, must have been much poorer than the one which built the large marble-lined Imperial Palace.

Interpretation of Special Features

One problem that arose from the study concerned the possible use of the unoccupied space in the right-front corner of some Mithraea. Such an unexplained space is present in the Serpents, Lucretius Menander,[20] Baths of Mithra, Porta Romana, and Painted Walls. Although there are indications that there were once doorways at the right front of the latter two Mithraea, it is highly probable that these doors were not used. Thus the problem remains of discovering how this space may have been employed.

The Mithraeum under San Clemente in Rome has a small stone bench in a similar space in the right-front corner. The bench was situated behind a screen-wall which hid it from the view of those reclining on the podia. The Sacello of the Three Naves at Ostia has a bench in the same area. It is possible that a similar bench occupied this space in the Ostian Mithraea and that it had a liturgical function. It is also possible that this space was a liturgical station even if it contained no such seat.

The use of the floor-level podia niches also constitutes a problem. Were they used to hold lamps or offerings or statues? A small I-shaped altar was found firmly cemented into one of the floor niches of the Seven Doors. Did niches in other sanctuaries contain such altars? It is difficult to accept this explanation because the niches in the Seven Spheres were hollowed on the bottom as if to hold some sort of liquid. It seems probable that their use varied from Mithraeum to Mithraeum.

It is sometimes extremely difficult to determine whether a room adjacent to a Mithraeum was employed by the cult. Becatti and others indicate that the room behind the front wall of Lucretius Menander was not so used. However, an examination of the site reveals a break in the left part of the front wall which might have been a doorway at one time. Behind this break

20. *Ve-Corp*, I, Inscr. 224, mentions this space but does not interpret its meaning. The plan in *Be-Mi*, p. 19, does not show an exit door at this point even though there is a break in the wall. An examination of this break indicated it was not an antique doorway for the Mithraeum.

is a room which can be entered only through the sanctuary.[21] It seems at least possible that the room could have been used for Mithraic purposes. The courtyard directly adjacent to the Mithraeum of the House of Diana might have been used similarly by the Mithraists.[22] This courtyard, which has been sealed off from the rest of the building, communicates with the Mithraeum by means of small holes in the left wall of the main room. Both sanctuaries indicate that these adjacent areas could have been employed by those who frequented the sanctuaries.

It is interesting to note that three of the Mithraea are divided by partitions which partially cut off the back section of the podia from the front section. Thus in the House of Diana, when the podia were installed to run from one room of the apartment to the other, the wall dividing the two rooms was not removed. Consequently the podia have been cut in two, although a small doorway was made in the right dividing wall to enable one to walk the length of the right podium.

The podia of the Baths of Mithra are divided into front and rear sections in a similar manner. The effect of this is to make the rear section of the podia appear less important than the front section. Such a structural division occurs again in the Painted Walls, where a cross-wall has been partly removed to provide a space for the central aisle. At the Painted Walls, as at the other Mithraea, such a cross-wall does not seem to be structurally necessary. It is therefore probable that it served a symbolic purpose. The twofold structural division probably corresponds to the liturgical division of higher and lower grades of initiation.[23] The division of the mosaic floor of the Planta Pedis by a cross-band of black mosaic and the division of the floor of Lucretius Menander by a band of small white-marble blocks highlight this relation of both structure and decoration to Mithraic liturgy.

A question must be raised concerning the use of the bema. Some look as if they provided a seat for an official of the cult. The top step of the

---

21. The plan in *Be-Mi*, p. 19, does not indicate a doorway at this point.
22. *Be-Mi*, p. 11, indicates no such usage.
23. *Cu-Mi*, p. 155.

aedicula of the House of Diana, the fifth (final) step of the bema of
the Imperial Palace, and the bema of the Painted Walls may have served this
function. The bema of Santa Prisca in Rome has a clearly discernible seat;
in addition, there is a *thronos* built into the right bench. Perhaps the Ostian
bemas may even have been symbolic thrones for the god.[24]

The use of the large central altar poses a problem. It was surely used
for offering sacrifices to the god; but it is not clear what kinds of sacrifices
were offered or in what way they were offered. Remaining monuments
provide clues for possible uses. In the museum at Ostia there is, on one side of
a triangular candelabrum, a relief of a satyr offering a sacrifice on an
I-shaped altar. The satyr holds a cornucopia over the fire. Another relief
shows a Silenus making an offering.[25] On top of the altar are burning wood
faggots, a pomegranate, and other assorted fruits. Such fruit offerings
may have been made on the altars of Mithra. Perhaps small birds were also
offered, since such bones were found in a podium niche of the Planta Pedis.[26]
It is also probable that the small altars affixed to the ends
of the podia were used for fire.

Finally, the problems raised by the basins set into the floors of the
aisles remain unanswered. Were these basins used for the ritual baptism
known to be practiced in Mithraism?[27] Did the worshipers of Mithra wash
their hands before offering prayer, as the Jews did? Did the basins
contain anything besides water, or were they meant to
symbolize the sacred stream of Mithraism?[28]

In this chapter I have attempted to sketch out the basic outlines of

24. See *VE-Prisc*, pp. 126–28, in which it is argued that the builders (and perhaps
also the painters) who enlarged Santa Prisca were influenced by the Painted Walls
at Ostia. The authors suggest that at the Painted Walls the Father may have sat on the
throne, at which time he may have been adored as the sun-god.

25. R. Calza and M. Squarciapino, *Museo Ostiense* (Rome: Istituto Poligrafico
dello Stato, 1962), satyr: p. 43, no. 18 (12); Silenus: p. 41, no. 12 (141).

26. *Ve-Corp*, I, Inscr. 272.

27. *Cu-Mi*, p. 157.

28. Porphyry *De antro nympharum* 18.

the Ostian Mithraeum and to deal with certain specialized questions raised by physical peculiarities of the sanctuaries. It is from such highly specialized and technical inquiry that the more broadly interpretative essays which follow were developed. These, then, are the data. Now, what do they mean?

The Environment of

Ostian Mithraism

JOHN SCHREIBER

THE ATTEMPT to set Ostian Mithraism within the historical context afforded it by the social and economic development of the city of Ostia is attended by all of the difficulties which normally arise when we try to reconstruct history from fragments of evidence. Viewed from a purely sociological vantage point, Ostian Mithraism is a subculture in Ostian society. As such it is both determined by Ostia and plays a role in the formation of Ostia.

The difficulties of historical reconstruction lie on both sides of this equation. Regarding Mithraism, there are only architectural and artistic remains and some accompanying inscriptions. There are few texts by which to interpret these remains or to give insight into the genius and the appeal of this religion. Regarding Ostia, we are more fortunate. To be sure, the dates of its settlement and abandonment are not precisely known. But from the era of its prosperity and importance, a span of a few hundred years, there remain many architectural monuments, inscriptions, and records and a few texts regarding its role in the empire. (See Plates 6–12.) From these evidences we must seek to derive the history of a city and a religious movement within that city.

Toward this end the attempt will be made to describe the relationship between the Ostian Mithraea and their surroundings. Foremost among the problems encountered is that of assigning dates to structures in a city such as Ostia. This whole field is such a specialized one that it is often difficult to secure independent judgments as an adequate check on the reliability of the methodology.[1] In the case of the Mithraea the situation is further complicated because they make use of previously existing structures. Thus dating must often be based on alterations made in an existing structure when it was converted into a Mithraeum.

The first and most striking fact about the Mithraea in relation to the rest of the city is their even distribution.[2] In only one instance are there two Mithraea located in close proximity to each other, Lucretius Menander and the House of Diana. However, there is no other Mithraeum in the northern half of the city westward from these two until the Baths of Mithra, and if this entire quadrant of the city, with its probable heavy concentration of population, is considered to be the area served by the two Mithraea, there is no greater concentration of Mithraic sanctuaries in this region than elsewhere in the city.

What is really more amazing is the location of three Mithraea in the near eastern end of the city, where the resident population appears to have been rather small. The Mithraeum of the Seven Spheres, while located near a few small houses, is more prominently surrounded by the Grandi Horrea to the west, a large republican temenos extending to the south to the Decumanus Maximus, and the theater and Forum of the Corporations to the east. The area across the Decumanus to the south contains the two other Mithraea. There is also a large unexcavated sector of the city to the north; but even if this area is residential, there is apparently no easy means of access to

1. *Me* (pp. 554–57) has a good brief discussion of the problem of dating structures, with special reference to Ostian buildings.
2. See the map on p. 24. Cf. *Be-Mi* (p. 132).

23

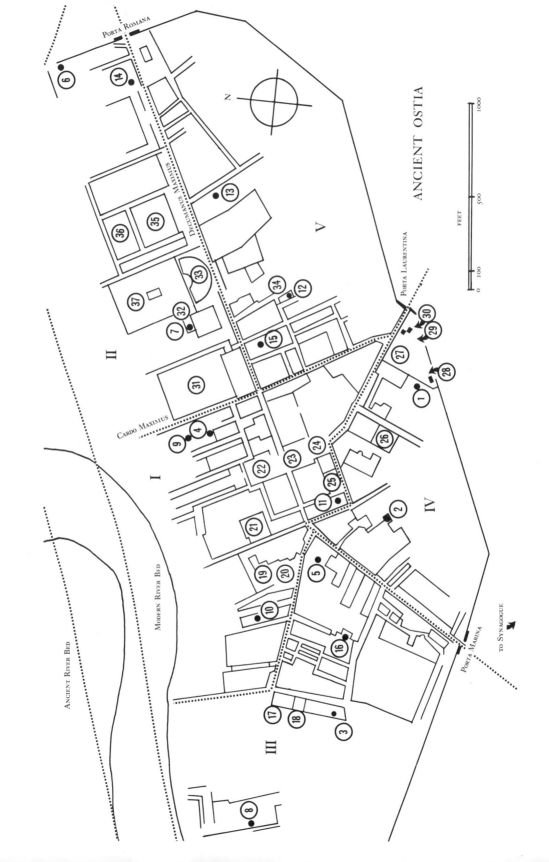

ANCIENT OSTIA

N

FEET

0 100 500 1000

Porta Romana

Ancient River Bed

Modern River Bed

Decumanus Maximus

Cardo Maximus

Porta Laurentina

Porta Marina

to Synagogue

I

II

III

IV

V

6

14

13

36

35

33

37

32

7

31

34

12

15

9

4

30

29

27

28

1

26

24

23

22

25

11

2

21

19

20

5

10

16

17

18

3

8

Other structures mentioned in text

17 House of Bacchus and Ariadne
18 Serapeum
19 House of Amor and Psyche
20 Temple of Hercules
21 Horrea of Epagathiana and Epaphroditiana
22 Capitol
23 Forum
24 Temple to Roma and Augustus
25 Round Temple (Pantheon or Augusteum)
26 House of the Fishes
27 Magna Mater Temenos
28 Temple of Magna Mater
29 Temple of Attis
30 Temple of Bellona
31 Grandi Horrea
32 House of Apuleius
33 Theater
34 Bona Dea Temple
35 Baths of Neptune
36 Firemen's Barracks
37 Forum of the Corporations

Mithraea

1   Animals
2   Seven Doors
3   Planta Pedis
4   House of Diana
5   Painted Walls
6   Aldobrandini
7   Seven Spheres
8   Imperial Palace
9   Lucretius Menander
10 Baths of Mithra
11 Fructosus
12 Felicissimus
13 Sabazeo
14 Porta Romana
15 Serpents
16 Three Naves

PLATE 6   Mars

PLATE 7   The House of Amor and Psyche

PLATE 8   The House of Apuleius

PLATE 9   The Capitol

29

PLATE 10   Mosaic from the House of Bacchus and Ariadne

PLATE 11   Horrea Epagathiana et Epaphroditiana

PLATE 12   Mask in Stone from the Theater

the vicinity of the Mithraeum of the Seven Spheres entrance from the north.

The Sabazeo and Porta Romana sanctuaries are located in the extreme eastern section of the city, on opposite sides of the Decumanus Maximus. Both are closely related to warehouses—Sabazeo is in a *horrea* complex, and Porta Romana occupies a space which appears originally to have been a corridor flanking a warehouse. There is no residential building at all in the surrounding excavated area south of the Decumanus, nor is there any sign of any significant amount of housing to the north. In fact, the Porta Romana Mithraeum is surrounded on three sides by horrea, baths, and shops. There are a few small houses just inside the city gate. Farther to the north, where there could have been houses in the area yet unexcavated, there was another Mithraeum, the Aldobrandini sanctuary.

Thus, in the distribution of the Mithraea, there are two facts which demand consideration. One is the even pattern of distribution as a whole. The other is that this distribution extends even to areas which contain little observable housing. It is impossible to overemphasize the importance of this distribution of Mithraea throughout the city. No other Ostian cult, Roman or Eastern, offers any real parallel for such a distribution of cult sanctuaries. The proliferation of Mithraea suggests two things: first, that Mithraic communities preferred to remain relatively small, and additional sanctuaries were added as the number of adherents grew; and second, that each sanctuary drew its adherents from a more or less compact area in its immediate vicinity.

Expressing these conclusions only serves to increase the puzzle presented by the existence of Mithraea in relatively nonresidential areas. It could be argued that these Mithraea are simply for the use of the rather small resident population in the vicinity, but the disproportionately high number of Mithra-worshipers in the eastern section of the city would then call for explanation.

Perhaps the Mithraea were placed so that their surroundings would be largely deserted at their time of use, as a means of enhancing their arcane nature. Indeed, Meiggs implies that, insofar as imperial usage was concerned, Ostian horrea were abandoned in favor of Portus about the middle of the third century.[3] Unfortunately the archaeological evidence does not permit the precise establishment of the chronological relationship of these events.[4] However, in the midst of the decline of both wealth and population which would have followed Ostia's demise as an imperial storehouse, it is unlikely that a religion such as Mithraism, already having a dozen or more widely scattered sanctuaries, would have wanted or needed or been able to establish more sanctuaries.

It is more likely that these sanctuaries were used precisely at those times when an area composed of horrea and baths would be in greatest use. The areas containing sanctuaries such as Planta Pedis and the Baths of Mithra would also have been dominated by the presence of dock and warehouse workers. Some of these sanctuaries may have taken their worshipers from among the men who worked in the warehouses rather than from the persons who actually lived in the area.[5]

With regard to the buildings in the immediate vicinity of Mithraea, no real pattern emerges from the data.[6] Every major type of structure appears. No type of building seems essential, and none is avoided. In the vicinity of most of the Mithraea are other religious sanctuaries of some type. This is not significant, however, because temples and religious shrines are extremely numerous in Ostia, and there does not seem to be an affinity for any particular deity.

When the actual buildings in which the Mithraea are located are considered, the range is more limited. All Mithraea occupy previously existing structures; no building in Ostia was built to house a Mithraeum. Nine of the fourteen Mithraea studied are located either in houses or in what were originally shops, in buildings which also included housing. Of these,

3. *Me*, pp. 308-9.

4. A major difficulty with the third century is that there are fewer inscriptions, probably due to economic factors, and that dating is even more difficult because of the absence of dated brickstamps and the re-use of old material.

5. We must be cautious about assigning too great importance to distances to be traversed between places of residence and Mithraea, since no distance is too great in Ostia; nevertheless, the distribution of sanctuaries does suggest that they aim at serving persons in a compact area.

6. For a synopsis of the data, see the chart on pp. 42–45.

three were clearly insulae; one (Painted Walls) was originally a domus; one
was a large villa, and the other four were *caseggiati*. The plan of the House
of the Painted Walls had already been altered before the installation of
the Mithraeum; thus there may be no justification for referring to this building
as a "domus" at the time the Mithraeum originated. The other sanctuary
which is in close proximity to a domus is that of the Seven Spheres,
but it bears a closer relation to the row of shops extending westward from the
domus, of which it was probably originally one. At the time Mithraea were
coming into existence, there were probably very few domus-type houses
in Ostia. They had given way to make room for structures which used space
more economically, in the face of Ostia's second-century population explosion.
The domus-type again gains the ascendancy in the late third and fourth
centuries, but by this time no new Mithraic sanctuaries are appearing. The
so-called "Imperial Palace" (Plate 13) is a fairly large complex, which
in antiquity would have been located near the mouth of the river. It could
have been an official residence or a private villa. Those Mithraea which
were not in houses or shops include one in the underground service area of a
bathing establishment, three which were in or connected with
horrea, and one in the cella of a collegiate temple.

If we try to characterize the neighborhoods surrounding Mithraea on the
basis of the type of housing they exhibit, we again encounter the entire
range of possibilities. Indications are that neighborhoods in Ostia were not
economically homogeneous. Further, even in the wealthiest neighborhoods
there would have been slaves, shopkeepers, and others of lesser social
rank. Thus conclusions as to the class of persons attracted to
Mithra ultimately must rest on other grounds than the type of
housing in the vicinity of Mithraic sanctuaries.

A word must also be said regarding the inscriptional evidence found in
the Mithraea.[7] All together, approximately twenty-one different names appear
in the inscriptions from the fourteen Mithraea studied. Four of the names
are probably of slaves (Pyladen at Planta Pedis; Diocles at Lucretius
Menander; Felicissimus at Felicissimus [Plate 3]; and Fructus at Sabazeo).

7. *Ve-Corp*, I, 114–47.

35

That this proportion of names recorded in the inscriptions should belong to slaves seems highly significant, even considering the small size of the sample. More important, all of the names in the inscriptions probably belong to freedmen or descendants of freedmen whose families originated in other parts of the empire. Occasionally, as in the case of M. Caerellius Hieronymus (Animals and House of Diana), there is evidence that the person in question was a man of some means. The same name appears in an inscription dated to 198 A.D., from which it appears that he belonged to the *collegium fabrum tignuarium*, a guild of builders which appears to have been one of the largest and wealthiest in Ostia.[8] Otherwise, the inscriptional evidence gives little indication of persons of wealth or position among the Ostian devotees of Mithra. Meiggs points out that no official or magistrate of the city is known to have participated in the cult.[9] However, some persons of means must have been a part of or friendly to Mithraic communities in order to secure the use of space in private buildings for Mithraic sanctuaries. There must have been either participants in the cult or patrons who were willing to give or purchase space for Mithraic use and to pay for the necessary structural and decorative adjustments in the room.

Another noteworthy phenomenon exhibited by these sanctuaries vis-à-vis their surroundings is the arcane nature of the sanctuaries. In only two cases—Planta Pedis and Seven Spheres—is it possible to step directly from a street into a Mithraeum. As has been pointed out in the preceding paper, in no case is a Mithraeum located on a major thoroughfare. They are to the rear of houses, off small alleys, off courtyards of horrea, and in similar out-of-the-way locations. In at least one case—Felicissimus—a door connecting the Mithraeum with the street has been walled up.

When the Mithraea are arranged in approximate chronological order, two other interesting results emerge. Of those Mithraea available to us for study, the Mithraeum of the Animals appears to be the earliest. It is dated by Becatti *ca.* 160 A.D. Vermaseren records altar inscriptions in this

8. This conclusion is strengthened by the fact that among the recorded occupations of the *severi Augustales*, the guild most often mentioned is this one.

9. *Me*, pp. 373–74.

36

PLATE 13   The Imperial Palace Mithraeum

37

area datable to 142–43 A.D. in connection with this Mithraeum.[10] These inscriptions make no reference to Mithra or to Mithraic functionaries but appear to belong to the adjoining Magna Mater temenos rather than to the Mithraeum. The only other sanctuary which has been dated to the 160's is the Mithraeum of the Seven Doors. It is in the same section of the city and is the sanctuary closest to the Animals; thus Mithraism seems to have originated in this south-central sector of the city.[11] While there is no direct evidence for any connection, it may be more than coincidence that the two earliest Ostian Mithraea are located in the quarter of the city which also included the Magna Mater–Attis–Bellona temenos.[12]

The further spread of Mithraism in the city seems to have been marked by two clear stages. In the first, which occupies the rest of the second and the early years of the third century, Mithraism spreads rapidly through the area north of the Decumanus Maximus and west of the theater and Forum of the Corporations (Region III, the section of Region I north of the Decumanus, and the section of Region II west of the theater). Most of this area, especially in Regions I and III, was heavily populated. In the next stage, which extends for an indefinite span of time in the third century, Mithraism appears in the central section of the city, south of the Decumanus; in Region V, which comprises the southeastern quadrant of the city; and east of the Forum of the Corporations.

There exists one exception to this pattern, the Aldobrandini Mithraeum at the northeastern gate of the city near the river. This exception is to be understood in terms of that area's proximity to the river. Sociologically the area may have had more in common with other sections of the city which also lay along the river, where Mithraism spread in the late second century, than with the area along the Decumanus near the Porta Romana.

One other pattern emerges when the Mithraea are viewed in their

10. *Ve-Corp*, I, Inscrs. 285–86.

11. The question of which Mithraeum was the earliest in Ostia must be answered with the clear understanding that new excavations could provide a new answer. There were almost certainly Mithraea at Ostia which have not yet been found.

12. As Cumont noted, this is a graphic archaeological demonstration of the close relation between Mithra and Cybele which is suggested by the bull-killing imagery that appears in both (*Cu-Mi*, p. 179).

chronological sequence. Here the chronological point at which a line may be drawn is not perfectly clear because of the roughness of the dating of the sanctuaries. For purposes of discussion, those Mithraea which may have originated in the second century will be considered below as one group and those which seem clearly to have originated in the third as another.

In the first group there are seven sanctuaries. Of these, five are clearly either in houses or in shops—located on private property. Another (Seven Doors) occupies one room in a horrea. Most Ostian horrea were probably under either imperial ownership or imperial control. The horrea in which this Mithraeum is located, however, is quite small, comprising only six rooms. It is located in the part of town farthest from the river, and there is not even a street which approaches it from the direction of the river. Thus it could have had no relationship to the dock area or the imperial cargoes received there and is most likely to have been privately owned and operated. The seventh Mithraeum in this earlier grouping is that in the Imperial Palace. The use of this complex of buildings is debated by scholars. Chronologically, however, the Imperial Palace Mithraeum stands at the dividing point between the two groups, appearing in the late second or early third century. Thus at least six and perhaps all seven of these earlier seven sanctuaries are located on private property.

When we turn to the seven in the second group, we find that four do not fit the earlier pattern.[13] Two are located in, or in close connection with, large horrea. Meiggs discusses the issue of imperial control in Ostia at some length. He examines the references in the inscriptional evidence to various imperial officials and concludes that "the procurator was responsible for the maintenance of granaries and other warehouses used at Ostia and the harbours for Roman supplies."[14] The probability is that large complexes of horrea were either owned by or were under the close supervision of the imperial government. Another sanctuary is in the underground service area of a set of baths. Most large bathing establishments are assumed to have been public, probably operated by the city. A fourth Mithraeum in this group

13. There is some question about the Mithraic nature of the Sabazeo sanctuary, but, even if it is excluded, three of the six later Mithraea are not on private property.
14. *Me*, p. 300.

appears in a collegiate temple, in the place where we would normally
expect to find a temple either to the emperor cult or to more traditional
Roman deities.[15] As Meiggs notes, from Augustus onward "the guilds
remained subject to central control. To maintain a secure existence every guild
had to have the formal sanction of the Roman Senate or emperor."[16] In the
late empire, as economic problems increased, there was also increasing
regulation of guild activities. It is difficult to imagine either Senate or emperor
sanctioning or ignoring the cult of a foreign deity, installed on the premises
of an imperially chartered organization, replacing the official and traditional
Roman cults, in the first two centuries of the empire. Yet, this is exactly
what has occurred in the Fructosus Mithraeum in the third century.[17]

What did this mean for the city of Ostia and for the cult of Mithra?
There is no evidence that Mithraism was ever forced to hide or that it suffered
persecution. Nor is there clear evidence that it received any official status
in the third century. It does appear clear, however, that there was a time when
the cult either preferred or was forced to utilize private premises. At a later
time it gained access to several structures which were public or were
under imperial supervision. Sociologically speaking, Ostian society
began to integrate into the mainstream of its life what had
previously been a relatively hidden subculture.

As for the cult of Mithra, its arcaneness was compromised. As Professor
Laeuchli will show in his second paper, arcaneness has several dimensions, one
of which is sociological. In the third century the inside of a Mithraeum
may have been as hidden as ever. Its cultic acts and rituals were probably as
secret as ever. Sociologically, however, Mithraism had become more
visible in Ostian society; and to the extent that one dimension
of its arcaneness was lessened, the entire psychological effect of
hiddenness was compromised. Insofar as this was involved in the strength
and the appeal of the religion, any weakening of it would contribute
to the weakening of Mithraism's entire appeal.

15. *Me*, p. 327.
16. *Me*, p. 311.
17. Also in this connection, it is interesting that the Mithraeum of the Serpents
stands in place of an earlier *lararium*.

In summary, several conclusions emerge from this study of the Mithraic communities of Ostia. First, the Mithraea by the late third century are rather evenly distributed through the city. This distribution extends even to areas that are very sparsely populated because of large complexes of baths, horrea, and the like. Perhaps some sanctuaries were also frequented by the men who worked in such areas rather than residents of the vicinity only.

Second, the available evidence suggests that Mithraea drew their adherents primarily from the slave and freedman population and their descendants. The mushrooming of sanctuaries in the last decades of the second and early years of the third centuries in the areas of heaviest population suggests that the religion appealed to those persons who comprised the bulk of the Ostian population—persons who drew their sustenance from the work at the docks and in the warehouses of Ostia. While there were probably a few men of some means, wealth and political power probably were not widespread among the followers of Mithra.

Third, the locations of the Mithraea emphasize the arcane nature of the cult. Existing structures which could be converted to the basic Mithraic plan of side benches and center aisle, which were not located on a main street, and which were located in such a way that the activities inside could be hidden from the outside world were acceptable for use as Mithraea.

Fourth, as to the rise and spread of the cult, it seems to have had its start in the south-central section of the city in the same area with the Magna Mater temenos. Next it spread to the heavily populated western, northwestern, and north-central sections of the city, which lay toward the river and the coast. Finally it was established in the southeastern and eastern sections of the city.

Fifth, there seems to be a development from early location of Mithraic sanctuaries solely in privately owned buildings to a later stage when buildings subject to public or imperial supervision could be used. Furthermore, in two cases (Fructosus and Serpents), Mithraea stand in places which would normally house or had earlier housed the shrines of traditional Roman deities. This development may have resulted in the loss of some of the sense of mystery or hiddenness involved in participation in the cult's activities. Such a loss may have contributed to the decreasing appeal of the cult and may have been a factor in its decline.

41

Mithraeum	Location*	Date of Mithraeum†	Type of Building	Date of Building
Animals	IV, ii, 11	*ca.* 160	Insula	Trajanic period
Seven Doors	IV, v, 13	160–70	Horrea	Early 1st century
Planta Pedis	III, xvii, 2	176–80	Caseggiato	Hadrianic period
House of Diana	I, iii, 3	Late 2nd century	Insula	Antonine period
Painted Walls	III, i, 6	Late 2nd century	Caseggiato	Built: 2nd century B.C. Restored: 1st century B.C., 1st, 2nd century A.D.
Aldobrandini	II, i, 2	End 2nd century	Area unexcavated	
Seven Spheres	II, viii, 6	Late 2nd–early 3rd centuries	Shop or caseggiato	Hadrianic period
Imperial Palace	III	Late 2nd–early 3rd centuries	Villa or public bldg.	Antonine and late 2nd century
Lucretius Menander	I, iii, 5	Early 3rd century	Insula	Hadrianic period
Baths of Mithra	I, xvii, 2	Early 3rd century	Baths	Hadrianic period
Fructosus	I, x, 4	Mid-3rd century	Collegiate temple	222–35

* The references locate the structure in the city according to the divisions made by the excavators; maps showing these divisions may be found in any of the standard sources cited in these studies, such as *To, Me.*

ENTRY	NEARBY BUILDINGS
From Via della Caupona; through buildings in block to southern corner; enter Mithraeum through parallel corridor	Houses; shops; fullonica; mill; baths; Magna Mater temenos; Attis and Bellona sanctuaries
Enter courtyard of horrea via small street from south	Houses; shops; baths; unexcavated area
From small street which ends shortly to south	Houses; baths; horrea; public building; Serapeum
Through the insula	Houses; shops; mill; lararium; Lucretius Menander Mithraeum
From Via della Foce; through alley or corridor and courtyard of house to entrance	Houses; shops; baths; public building; Temple of Hercules
Area unexcavated	Area unexcavated
From small street behind republican temenos	Houses; shops; horrea; unexcavated area; theater; Forum of Corporations; republican temenos
Area unexcavated	Area unexcavated
Through house or from street via corridor	Houses; shops; mill; horrea; unexcavated; House of Diana Mithraeum
Via rear entry to underground service area	Houses; shops; horrea; guild; unexcavated area; Temple of Hercules
Via courtyard of building	Houses; shops; fullonica; "Round Temple"

† Dates of Mithraea are those assigned in *Be-Mi;* those of structures are as indicated in *To.* The only exception is the Mithraeum of the Imperial Palace, in which case Vermaseren's dating has been followed (*Ve-Corp*, I, 127).

Mithraeum	Location*	Date of Mithraeum†	Type of Building	Date of Building
Felicissimus	V, ix, 1	Mid-3rd century	Shop or caseggiato	Mid-3rd century
Sabazeo	V, xii, 3	Mid-3rd century	Horrea	120–25
Porta Romana	II, ii, 5	3rd century	Corridor of horrea	Hadrianic period
Serpents	V, vi, 6	Mid- or late 3rd century	Shop or caseggiato; lararium	Hadrianic period

44

ENTRY	NEARBY BUILDINGS
From adjoining room, which opens to small dead-end street	Houses; shops; baths; fullonica; unexcavated area; Bona Dea temenos
From courtyard of horrea	Horrea; shops; baths; houses
From room to north, which opens onto small street flanking the horrea	Horrea; shops; baths; unidentified shrine
From small passageway reached by alley from north or small street from south	Houses; shops; guild

45

Mithraic Dualism

SAMUEL LAEUCHLI

THE MITHRAIC DISCOVERIES at Ostia make us seek anew for the secret of Mithra's impact on the Roman world. What gave to the rapidly increasing *Sol Invictus* worship its spectacular impetus, spectacular both in terms of the short span of time during which it rose and in terms of the urban territory it embraced? Something must have spoken deeply to the men of Ostia. Isis was in the town; Magna Mater was worshiped; Bellona had her temple. But Mithra had spread into practically every neighborhood and outshone them all. We want to explain this impact under the summary term "Mithraic dualism," specifying the cultural, religious, and communal ramifications of this concept.

The Symbol and the Myth

We begin with an obvious observation. The Mithraic cult contained a language of symbols which were certainly not inherently Mithraic. When a

lararium was transformed into a Mithraeum, its snakes (Plate 14)—
widespread symbol of fertility—could be retained without hesitance.[1] The
same holds true for the half-moon or pine cone, scorpion or dog, *krater*
or flaming torch. In the floor mosaic of Felicissimus, practically every symbol
can be documented by other religious or nonreligious parallels, as, for
instance, the thunderbolt (Plate 15), the sistrum (Plate 16), the staff of
initiation, or the diadem of Venus.[2] A man did not find new
symbolism when he entered the Mithraic sanctuary.

When a city became fascinated by a new religion which used such
commonplace symbolism, the symbolism cannot be held responsible for the
success of that religion. A wild syncretistic sect can lead us astray into
an analysis of, and speculation about, this or that specific symbol. To be sure,
the symbols—the bull and the raven and the sun—had their place in
the cult; but something in the use of these symbols must have exerted
a fascination. To find a drove of Oriental and domestic symbols in the
imagery of a cult was surely no strange sight to anyone in this utterly
syncretistic culture.[3] (See Plates 17–19.)

One must point instead to the myth to which the specific symbols were
subservient. This myth is known to some extent, even in some of its
variations.[4] Mithra, sent by the sun, was born of a rock; he captured and later
slew a bull while holding its nostrils. Out of the bull's dead body rose new
life. Mithra, after a final banquet with Sol, went up to heaven; from there he
helped the initiated. Related to this basic myth was a whole cosmogony
and theology, taught by priests throughout the empire and containing
elements that had been acquired as the Mithraic myth traveled through
Mesopotamia toward the Mediterranean world. Interesting as they are in
research, many problems of syncretistic details (cosmogony; the
leontocephalous god; Celsus' "Mithraic" elements) are peripheral to an
understanding of the Persian cult's impact upon a Roman town such

---

1. *Be-Mi*, p. 103; *Sq*, p. 52.
2. *Be-Mi*, pp. 105 ff.; *Sq*, pp. 52–54.
3. *Sq*, pp. 60 ff.
4. *Cu-Mi*, pp. 104 ff.

47

PLATE 14   Snake (from the Mithraeum of the Planta Pedis)

PLATE 15   Thunderbolt (from the Mithraeum of Felicissimus)

PLATE 16   Sistrum

PLATE 17   Bull (from the Serapeum)

PLATE 18   Ibis (from the Serapeum)

PLATE 19   Inscription to Jupiter-Serapis

as Ostia Antica.[5] The center of the Mithraic theology was the
myth itself and what it stood for, and not any cosmological, philosophical,
or religious ideas independent of it.

But now we have to raise the question again: in what lay the newness?
The Mithra cult symbol itself was nothing totally new; one frequently can
find winged victories slaying bulls in the Mithraic gesture.[6] Furthermore,
a great many Eastern cult myths plead for the soul of Roma and offered
rebirth, new life, and immortality in the context of initiation. Why should a
Roman accept Mithra over Isis or Cybele? We cannot solve this question
by merely pointing to the soldiers who were supposed to have brought the
Persian cult to the West. Even if that is originally true, it does not explain
Ostia (and with it the urban Mithraism) in the least, because one cannot
explain the urban success via soldiers. When, on the other hand, we postulate
two bearers of this religion, the merchant and the soldier, we have said
very little, because in this case Mithra fulfilled two clearly distinct roles. The
success of Mithra in Ostia could not have been due to the cult qua cult, to its
symbolism or its theology, but to *the way* the cult and symbol took hold of
Ostia. That which opened the homes, baths, and granaries to the god with the
Phrygian cap was as much the context in which the cult appeared at Ostia
as the cult itself. The *original* meaning of the cult and the *concrete* meaning
of the cult are two different matters when a cult becomes a part of history.

The Symbolization

In order to understand the myth's meaning we proceed to a second
phenomenon. Popular notions to the contrary, we are convinced that in the
Mithraea of Ostia no bulls were ever killed. Whether in Trèves or in the Baths
of Caracalla actual *taurobolia* were held does not concern us here; it was
certainly not the case in the sanctuaries of Ostia. They are much too small
for such a ritual and much too numerous for such expensive sacrifices. It would

5. *Cu-Mi*, pp. 11–32.
6. Cf. the Acropolis-type Nike in Reinhard Lullies, *Greek Sculptures* (New York,
1957), p. 191.

have been necessary to lead the bull through the living room or corridors
of houses in order to reach the place of immolation, and any struggle before
his death would have played havoc with the mosaics as well as with the
delicate benches.[7] The entrances were small, and the spaces around the altars
obviously made no provision for such a liturgical event. All we need to do
is compare these house churches with the one place that might have served for
the taurobolia, i.e., the fortress-like ditch in the Sullan tower.[8] The
tauroboliati of Ostia were Magna Mater initiates and not Mithraic ones,
and not one inscription either by or to a Mithraic *Pater*
mentions the baptism by blood.

But here the problem becomes acute: we face a cult myth, the major
representation of which portrays the killing of the bull—and then no killing
takes place! We must imagine Ostia in its daily life where such public
bull-killing was not as alien as it seems to the modern reader outside Spain.
Not only were taurobolia enacted in the rite of Cybele; the *immolatio boum*
was carried out in Roman ceremonies, as the floor mosaics in the Firemen's
Barracks exemplify.[9] If the slaying of a bull had been a major event for
the twenty Mithraea, there would have been ways to achieve it; and—parallel
to the Cybele inscriptions—we would surely find archaeological traces in
dedications. Instead, we find the Mithra-worshiper concerned with a
cult myth that was no longer re-enacted physically.

The answer is clear, of course: by the time Mithra reached Ostia the
taurobolium had become symbolic. Parallel to the symbolization in the cults
of Dionysus and in the spiritualization of the Old Testament, the ancient
cultic practice had been transformed into a spiritual, symbolic event. We are
witnessing again that significant transformation of the prehistoric natural
cults into their at times sophisticated, at times uncertain and tentative,

7. The popular-academic notion of a Mithraic blood bath (again in Cyril Eastwood,
Life and Thought in the Ancient World [Philadelphia, 1965], p. 181) does not stand
the archaeological evidence.

8. *Sq*, pp. 6–7; *Me*, p. 358. Cf. *C.I.L.*, XIV, 39 and Hilding Thylander, *Inscriptions
du Port d'Ostie* (Lund, 1952), p. 374.

9. Giovanni Becatti, *Scavi di Ostia*, Vol. IV, Pt. 1: *I Mosaici*, pp. 61–62 and Plate C.

"demythologizations." The slaughter of the bull now stands for something else; not merely does taurobolium mean something *in addition to* the act (which was always the case in any of the sacrificial rituals of ancient man), but now it means something *instead of* the act—a transmutation of vital importance for the history of ancient religions. That Mithra accepted the iconography of the winged victories in the act of slaying bulls shows that this process began the moment Mithraism entered the civilization of the Hellenistic world.[10] The iconographic *situs* of the tauroctonos in the axis of the sanctuary demonstrates that here lay the crucial symbol for this cult; while the *dendrophori* of Cybele still practiced the archaic rite, Mithra had turned symbolic.

The Identification

The symbolic transmutation of the cult myth, having begun centuries before it reached Ostia, poses a grave methodological problem. Originally, the slaying of the bull in the *spelaeum* belonged to a rural sphere of life from which meaning was easily obtained. Was not the daily existence part of a dying and revitalizing process, and thus was not Mithra a natural symbol for the daily life of his worshipers? The moment any symbolic transformation occurs, the original context breaks down. When the act is taken out of its naturalistic, archaic framework and transposed into "meaning," then this symbolic meaning depends upon the culture in which it is expressed. This is especially so when an archaic rural cult becomes urban, as was so obviously the case in Ostia's Mithraism. When the naturalistic cult myth of the Near East was transferred to the house sanctuaries of a Roman city, there occurred a profound transformation of meaning. This problem—so essential for an understanding of Christian history—must be faced at the outset of any research. Otherwise, any description of a myth's "original" astrological or cultic language may only cloud the issues instead of leading us to the heart of its life. The extent of Mithra's success at Ostia, over all its rivals, may not

---

10. *Cu-Mi*, p. 21; this does not deny regular small sacrifices, as is proved by the altars in the Mithraea, nor widespread magic practices (Luc. *Men.* 6).

have been due to its symbol itself—which surely did not differ so greatly from Syrian and Egyptian mystery patterns—but to the symbolic translation of its symbol and to the social forms in which this transformation took place.

To be sure, this problem confronts us with even greater obstacles. Because we must reckon with the possibility of such concrete symbolic transformation, the cult myth and its society may fulfill different roles in different parts of the world, and even within different strata of one town. The meaning of Mithraism in Syria, in Capua, and out on the Hadrian Wall may not be the same at all.[11] We may explain this by pointing to the profound difference between the meaning of Methodism at Aldersgate and in a large suburban Methodist Church. Furthermore, the process of symbolization may not have taken place everywhere with the same speed, and therefore symbolic transmutation was not homogeneous. It is quite possible that there were taurobolia now and then as archaic practices of the cult; and we find, symptomatically, that when the cult was entering its coma during the fourth century, the element of religious revival recurred in which the wheel of symbolization was turned back toward a Mithraic fundamentalism, i.e., a naturalistic, literalistic understanding of the myth. This is when we find evidences of actual bull-slaying.[12] We cannot hope to find a linear path of either the act of symbolization or the content of translation.

The conclusion of such remarks leads to the deduction that a Mithraic believer could receive more than one meaning from such a cult symbol. It is with this in mind that we want to ask about identification. With whom did an initiate, facing the tauroctonos during the ritual, identify? Three possibilities are open. In the first place, the identification could be with Mithra, the killer. Certainly the attraction of Mithraism to the soldier's psyche lay in this identification. It appears on several parallel levels outside

11. Not only was primitive Mithraism (Zend-Avesta, *Mihir-Yast* 35; *Ve-Corp*, I, pp. 8–9) far removed from Mithraism in the time of Pliny (*De fluv.* 23. 4), but Mithraism from the same period could differ radically in different parts of the ancient world, as can be shown by comparing the Santa Prisca inscriptions (*Ve-Prisc*, pp. 187 ff.) with the newly discovered text from eastern Iran (Helmut Humbach, *Die Kaniska-Inschrift von Surkh-Kotal* [Wiesbaden, 1960]).

12. *Ve-Corp*, I, Inscrs. 514, 515, 520, 522–24, 206, 420. All of these are from the fourth century, and most of them after A.D. 370!

Mithraism proper: in the *Invictus* of Aurelian fighting the Persians; in Constantine slaying Maxentius; in the identification with Hercules (as in the Herculi Invicto inscription of Ostia [see Plate 20]) or with Jupiter (as in the Invictus inscriptions of Diocletian).[13] Whether the killing of bulls was enacted regularly or not, the life of a soldier was one bitter or triumphant taurobolium.

A second identification centers on the bull. If we consider the lot of slaves in imperial society—a lot leading possibly to wealth, honor, and freedom but often, too, heaped with injustices and brutalities[14]—a slave's identification with the bull would have been a natural response. Such identification does not appear in inscriptions which focus on cult, *votum*, or practice; but as silent, emotional relation, as sympathy and response, it was indeed within the daily life of a servant. The slain animal was not evil; and, even in the myth itself, Mithra slew the bull reluctantly. But from the blood arose new life. A slave of Ostia found himself in the servile dimension of life; hence he would accept the myth differently from the shepherds of Persia, the king of Commagene, or the priests of Asia Minor. None of the former theologies could determine the sympathies and emotions of the slave. We understand how vital the distinction between a theology of the myth and the context of the myth becomes. That we must reckon with two possible identifications, here of the soldier and there of the slave, emphasizes the contextual significance as a myth receives its meaning, i.e., its translation.

The third possibility brings us, we believe, even closer to the Roman harbor at the mouth of the Tiber. The Mithraic initiate could identify with the total event. The whole was a drama which spoke to man; not this or that specific symbol, be it scorpion, bull, or Mithra; not this or that astrological or mythological statement accompanying the ritual. The whole event became symbolic victory—perhaps with man himself on both sides—a victory into which the believer was drawn as he participated, or at least tried to participate, in the rituals of preparation, initiation, and feasting. The

13. Cf. Giovanni Becatti, "Il culto di Ercole ad Ostia," *Bull. d. Comm. Arch. Comm. di Roma*, LXVII (1939), 37 ff.

14. Michael Grant, *The World of Rome* (New York, 1960), pp. 130 ff.

PLATE 20   Inscription to Hercules Invictus

representation of the bull-slaying became the symbol for what went on in the life of a Mithraic group. Here man was drawn into a victory, although he found himself in the midst of both Mithraic victory and the external Roman world. In this case, the detachment of the translation from the original cult meaning was carried to its extreme. While the first identification remained within a crude, naturalistic framework, the third identification had severed the ties with the naturalistic symbol and grasped instead the glorious symbolic impact of a solar strength, the *transmythologized invictus*.

We do not expect to find these three distinctions neatly separated in each instance. In the process of religious transformation a man can vacillate at different stages of his involvement. Because religion is not necessarily determined in one city by what it has been in another, the possibilities are many. Furthermore, in each city, the process of concretizing may have been a complex one. Do we not find at Ostia sanctuaries from the primitive level of Sabazeo to the relative wealth of the "Imperial" Palace?[15] It is therefore quite possible that a religion such as this would fulfill one role in one segment of the populace and another role in another segment. In such different identifications we find a possible explanation for Mithraism as a soldier's, a slave's, and a merchant's religion. The Mithraic symbol could be molded into different contexts; and by becoming concrete in these contexts, it changed its meaning.

It is above all the third hypothesis which interests us, not only because this is where the key to the Mithraic impact in Ostia may lie, but also because here we come to grips with the "Romanization" of an Eastern cult in the empire, a cult which understood how to play in a number of ways with the dualistic theme so prevalent in the last centuries of the ancient world.

The Dualistic Experience

The mystery religions had two dimensions. In a time of threatening cultural changes and an increasing amalgamation of indigenous cultures in the Mediterranean world, man longed to return to the earth, to the prehistoric

15. *Me*, p. 372; *Be-Mi*, pp. 53 ff. and 113 ff.

cycles of life and corn and death.[16] The rise of the mystery cults belonged to those centuries in which the loss of tribal, cultural, and religious security began. By return and by mysterious ritual, this security was offered to him again. Return and ritual appeared like two sides of a coin; in reality they contained a harsh theological, as well as existential, tension. In its origins the ritual was obviously naturalistic, from the slaying of the bull to the display of Eleusis and the ordeals under Cybele; but because man's natural existence was threatened, it was sought in a new setting. He joined the mystery because he had lost his world. At the heart of the mystery religions lies the rise of a dualistic experience.

The dualistic problem has been confused by two rigid assertions. The first limits dualism to an extreme of an Iranian type of two gods, one good and one evil. The second limits dualism to only the metaphysical, religious, or philosophical aspects of such duality. This narrow definition of dualism prevents the observer from grasping the dualistic problem in the ancient world. As Simone Pétrement has shown so well, when you say dualism—even in its philosophical and religious realms proper—you comprehend thereby an extensive scale of thought patterns—Plato, Valentinus, Mani—all three different from one another.[17] Only in the last type do we have ultimate dualism; but the first two show definite dualistic elements. The mysteries add a fourth dualistic type (qualified on the metaphysical plane, since only the scorpion is the product of Ahriman, and the bull is not evil)—a dualism that portrays the mythological event of killing, the struggle between Mithra and the bull.[18]

But the metaphysical consistency is only part of the dualistic problem. Throughout antiquity we find patterns of *social dualism*, as, for instance, in the Qumran community, in the initiation circle of the mysteries, or in

16. The early Mithraic texts are clearly naturalistic: *Sirozah* 2. 16; *Fravardin Yasht* 1. 18.

17. Simone Pétrement, *Le dualisme chez Platon, les gnostiques et les Manichéens* (Paris, 1947).

18. Plutarch understood this mixed dualism, so different from the Avestan texts (*Gah Haven* 2), when he described the Mithraic mediator between two forces (*De Isid. et Osir.* 46).

any exclusive community. There are clear ties between such social dualism and metaphysical dualistic thoughts (Mani), although the latter are often only partial (Qumran) or even peripheral (the *ekklesia*). There exists a *psychological dualism*. Man finds himself caught in an evil world, and he seeks for ways out of this existential impasse, by ascent, by acquiring magic formulas toward immortality, or by going through a ritual of rebirth. The relations between this dualism and the dualistic system are obvious in all the Gnostic constructions in which the existential dualism is brought into correlation with some form of cosmogony and a certain metaphysical theology. There is also an *ethical dualism*, which is detectable in the asceticism of the anchorites, in the castration rites of Magna Mater, or in the preparations for Mithraism. And, finally, we come to the *religious* and *philosophical* dualisms, which develop mythologies of two worlds, the poetry of the Fall and the patterns of salvation.

Placing these possibilities next to one another, we perceive immediately how they are related, although sometimes one is more in focus than another. The Manichaeans are supposed to be the "real" dualists of the fourth century, but they portray a social organization which in its dualistic form is closely related to other exclusive societies; while the Egyptian monks often lived a radical ethical dualism without daring to relate this ethical duality to monotheism and Christology. Dualism is therefore a phenomenon which comprises aspects of society and of the individual as well as of theology and cult.

At the core of the mystery experience lay a dualistic threat. Perhaps the rise of religion itself, in prehistoric times, was a first sign of this, when man dug his caves in Crete and Persia.[19] Yet, in such naturalistic religion man celebrated nature within nature, life within life; he was part of the cycle itself. The transformation of naturalistic religion into the mystery religions began as the cycle, the natural unity, began to give way. Awe turned into conquest; identification became withdrawal; natural participation became "participation" over against the natural habitat of religion and society. The

19. On the Aegean caves cf. George Thompson, *Studies in Ancient Greek Society* (London, 1949), pp. 231 ff. and 245–46.

cave became a house church—which meant a transformed house; the cultic formula was turned into an ascent to heaven; the rite of nature became the path toward immortality. Natural religion turned into mystery religion when the dualistic attack upon the natural experience of man forced him desperately to search for his roots. And therefore, what was originally natural re-enactment became artificially recreated re-enactment. The rite of Asia Minor's forests is transplanted into the *urbs* at the mouth of the Tiber.[20]

The "dualistic transformation" is understood as we look at the taurobolium itself. As we shall say in the final paper, we detect throughout the Mithraea of Ostia a modified arcane factor; the Mithraea were no longer actual caves, but they were partially hidden. Now the killing of the bull was surely no arcane event, either in Iran or in Italy! When the slaying of the bull became the symbolic representation for an arcane community, as in the Mithra reliefs, it was taken out of its original "Sitz im Leben," its natural context, and it expressed the myth of a community which through initiation and ritual separated itself from the rest of Ostia. In the Mithraea man experienced something which the "world" did not give him and which he also did not find in Roman paganism. The symbolization transplants the myth.

It is at this point that we begin to understand Mithra's impact on Ostia. Part of his attraction was surely the awakening of individuality in the offer of immortal life. This is what we called "psychological dualism," and the answers to it were found in Cybele and Isis as well as in Dionysus and Mithra. In Mithraism an additional fact appears, and it is the architectural evidence which reveals it: immortality was offered via Mithra in the form of a social experience. In the temple, even at the Pantheon near the Forum, the sacrificial ceremony was enacted on an altar outside; in Mithraism, the ritual took place in the secure house or in the baths and horrea. We can study the transition in the Cybele and Attis temples, the former being still a traditional temple with cella and external access, the latter beginning to close itself off, though still with a traditional shrine.[21] In Mithraism the sanctuary had become the house church; the temenos was closed in.

20. *Cu-Or*, pp. 46 ff., 204 ff.
21. *Sq*, pp. 4 ff.

63

This means that the Mithraic experience was a communal one, and in this communal dimension lay its impact on Ostia. In the house sanctuary with its initiation and myth the man of the seaport found a new home, a new people, a new identity. Here he was enclosed; here—in a somewhat separate world of his own—he feasted. The transformation of the collegiate temple into the Mithraeum of Fructosus furnishes the most telling evidence for the attraction which the communal mystery cult held for the city. Here, in a ritual of initiation, gradation, and feasting, slaves and merchants found a new communal experience. The cave became actually a new home; the ritual was an alternative to daily life; the banquet, vividly illustrated by the graffiti scratched into the plaster of the House of Diana, offered a new communal joy.[22] Individual search for immortality and gradual rise toward perfection were enacted by the circle of men assembling on the benches for ritual and feast. What the wealth of archaeological material displays above all is this communal dimension of the Mithraic experience.

We understand now the meaning of "dualism" within this urban, Romanized context. It is social dualism. On a metaphysical level it is exceedingly qualified, since the bull was slain but was not evil. Arcaneness was built into the brick and marble of a Roman port; and the initiated of Fructosus worshiped in the guild house of their profession. Yet, here lay the Mithraic attraction: to withdraw from the world into a closed-off circle that offered man both immortal life and a social unity. This was by no means a radical withdrawal. The merchants and slaves continued their business happily after finding communal and psychological satisfaction. It was the genius of this urbanized, Romanized Mithraism to offer man a new life by leaving him right where he was.

Here lay the issue between Christianity and Mithraism!

We understand the meaning of Mithraic dualism as we finally distinguish it from some of its rivals. It has become obvious that to understand Mithraism in terms of *naturalistic religion* would be to miss its impact on Roman society. While Paestum's holy city was enclosed by a temenos, the Mithraic

22. *Cu-Mi*, pp. 155 ff; *C.I.L.*, XIV, 5293; *Be-Mi*, p. 14.

partitions created an inner sanctuary, shutting out the outside world. The lararia were closed to the world. The whole naturalistic symbolism became mysterious, which means reserved for the circle. This step from the natural to the mysterious denotes the break with nature, at least with nature in the old pagan conception of it. Mithraism was only possible because something happened to the time-honored natural cycles of life.

The break with nature, however, was a qualified break. Mithraic dualism must be held separate from the Gnostic one. The latter possessed at times a similar symbolic language, as in the case of snake, water, and fire. But the Gnostics asked questions which neither soldiers nor worshipers dared to raise, questions about good and evil, which drove them to the familiar Gnostic doctrines of fall and redemption. Because of its theological depth, Gnostic dualism was much more intense; the world was seen in its terror, and the physical aspects of life were understood in their demonic nature. Mithra, as far as we can determine in retrospect, did not have a philosophy of religion; instead it had a myth and a cult. While the Gnostics had a theological, radical dualism, the Mithraists had a cultic one—nonphilosophical, considerably more bourgeois, and therefore more harmless; a social dualism related to the masonic ritual, which fits without conflict into the daily routine of a businessman. And yet, there is a tie between *gnosis* and the mystery cult, the first being the theology of the second, or—in reverse—the second being the practice of the first.[23] Because this practice was basically nontheological (see, e.g., the peripheral place of astrological or theological meaning in the Santa Prisca inscriptions), Mithraic dualism stopped short of both the acumen and the extremes in Gnostic thought. The man in Ostia did not join Mithra in order to find theology (this is where the Christian church as well as the Gnostics offered a profound alternative to Sol Invictus); rather, he found a myth in a communal context.

A final comparison could be made between Mithra and Plotinus, who, after all, lived in the Roman Campagna not far from Ostia. At first sight they

23. Hans Jonas, *Gnosis und spätantiker Geist* (Göttingen, 1954), Vol. II, Pt. 1, pp. 53–69.

65

seem as far apart as third-century Roman thought could be. Here a later Platonic philosophy of emanative monisms offers ascetic catharsis to the sophisticated intellectual; there a syncretistic Oriental mythology attracts the noisy, nonaristocratic Roman mob. But they resembled each other, both having a desire to escape from the world without admitting to a dualism either metaphysical or cultic. For both, that escape and its philosophical or cultic language were qualified, cautious, even unwilling; for one in an individualistic, for the other in a social, scheme. Just as neither scorpion nor bull were principles of evil (there is even an altar to Ahriman at Ostia), so matter and evil were declared nonexistent by Plotinus.[24] The latter would have protested at the very hint of such a comparison. But underneath the Plotinian monism lies the same dualistic threat which produced the arcaneness of a Mithraic circle at Ostia and the theological outcry of the Gnostic: Where do I come from and where do I go?[25] Mithraic dualism stands between the speculative theology of the Gnostics and the refined philosophy of Plotinus as a nonphilosophical Oriental cult with a myth it did not dare to question, a cult which offered a new psychological and communal experience to the tired and searching Hellenistic world. It is this Mithraic cult that found in Christianity its closest parallel and its worst enemy.

24. *C.I.L.*, XIV, 4311; Plot. *Enn.* III. 6. 6. Cf. Pliny's interpretation of Ahriman, *De Isid. et Osir.* 46.
25. Clem. Alex. *Exc. ex Theod.* 78. 2.

Reflections on the

Mithraic Liturgy

JERRY STEWARDSON
AND ERNEST SAUNDERS

THE SECRET RITES of the religion of Romanized Mithra have been an intriguing object of interest in ancient and modern times. The mysterious character of the Mithra cult stirred a curiosity in the heart of third-century man, and it evokes a kindred reaction in the mind of the historical investigator today. This ritual religion of redemption celebrated the victories won by the god of light who had challenged and overcome the darkness of this world. Positioned at the very center of the Mithraic riddle is the liturgy which remains, more than other aspects of this cult, almost impenetrable to the probings of the historical scholar. At this point of the investigation more than any other, the paucity of evidence about this secret cult is most apparent. Yet it is important that the investigator attempt to determine what the characteristics of the liturgy were, for the liturgy holds an important clue to the understanding of the entire phenomenon of Mithraism.

There were at least two types of Mithraic liturgies: the cult meal and the services of initiation, including the baptismal lustrations. In this paper we

shall concern ourselves mainly with the sacred meal celebrated in honor of
the invincible sun-god.[1] It may be, of course, that the meal was always
associated with the ceremonies of initiation. But there is no evidence
to identify it with entrance into any particular grade, and it is reasonable
to assume that worship of a noninitiatory sort was also practiced. As to the
several types of worship, the constitutive elements, the frequency of
observance, the significance of the zodiacal signs and the astronomical
order of the planets, and so forth, we know almost nothing.

The cult meal appears to have been the central rite in the cult's worship
life. Podia were constructed wide enough so that the participants could
recline—the characteristic Roman position for eating and entertaining. At
the top edge of the podia bordering on the central aisle was a shelf on
which, undoubtedly, food and drink were placed. (See Plate 4.) In many
artistic representations of the prototypical banquet between Sol and Mithra,
the gods appear reclining or seated together as they dine.

The pre-eminence of the cult meal is indicated in the iconography of the
cult as well as in its architecture. This holy banquet is portrayed in art
more often than any other scene in the mythology of Mithra except the
central tauroctonos (the bull-slaying scene). The mythological prototype of
the cult meal is the feast of Sol and Mithra before their ascent to heaven.
This scene occasionally occurs in the form of a relief on a reversible stone,
with a portrayal of the bull-slaying on the opposite side; an example of this is
seen in a relief found in Yugoslavia.[2] The relationship of the two scenes
also testifies to the prime importance of the meal in Mithraism. In
some paintings and reliefs, members of the cult are represented along with
Sol and Mithra, another clear indication that the mythology
was dramatized in the liturgy.

The banquet of Sol and Mithra is one scene in a sequence of actions
which effectualizes man's salvation. Mithra is the main god of the cult, yet,
at the same time, he and Sol together constitute a single theological entity, for

---

1. Cf. Justin, *Apol.* 1. 66.
2. *Ve-Corp*, II, Inscr. 1896, Figs. 490–91.

they represent the same divine reality. They are both solar divinities with some
interchangeable attributes, and both are involved in achieving redemption
for man. The nature of their relationship is hard for us to determine exactly;
in fact, its uncertainty constitutes one of the most difficult problems in
the investigation of Mithraism. The presence of the two sun-gods must have
resulted from a merging of two originally separate deities.[3]

Since the combined works of Mithra and Sol lie at the core of the cult's
mythology, it is highly probable that there was a certain continuity and
sequence in the various stories about the two gods. Since we know that part of
the mythology is imitated in the liturgical meal, it seems likely that the entire
cycle of stories about Sol and Mithra would also have been represented
in some way in the main liturgical ceremony. A viable method of approach,
therefore, is to understand the mythological events involving Sol and Mithra
as the basis for the liturgical structure. By studying the group of Sol-Mithra
pictorial representations, one can trace the structure of the main liturgy.

According to Cumont, the events involving the two gods began when
Mithra compelled Sol to render homage to him as a recognition of Mithra's
superiority and "to receive from him his investiture."[4] In so doing, Mithra
placed a crown on Sol's head and then concluded a covenant of friendship
with him. After this establishment of concord between the two, they
collaborated in killing the bull, celebrating a feast, and ascending to heaven in
Sol's chariot.[5] In art the following scenes are portrayed: (1) Sol kneels
before Mithra, (2) Mithra gives Sol his investiture, (3) the two make a pact
of agreement, (4) Mithra slays the bull with the collaboration of Sol, (5) the
two gods feast together, (6) they ascend together in a chariot. Although
the order given by Cumont may be the correct one, another sequence
is possible. The homage of Sol to Mithra and their resulting pact may have
taken place in the mythology *after* the bull-slaying. Therefore the sequence of
the stories would be: the bull-slaying, homage, investiture, pact, feast, and
ascent. This, of course, would give another interpretation to the stories.

3. *Ve-Mi*, p. 71.
4. *Cu-Mi*, p. 32.
5. *Ibid.*, pp. 132 ff.

The mythological order would indicate that Mithra killed the bull
at the command of Sol, who at this time held the supreme power, but that
Mithra, by his heroic deed, gained supremacy over Sol (as Ahura-Mazda
displaced Zervan in the Iranian myth, and Jupiter succeeded Saturn in Roman
mythology). Thus he humbles Sol and shows his power by crowning or
honoring him. Then the two gods form an alliance or pact before the feast.
They feast together in peace and finally ascend to heaven, where they
rule in unity. This suggested sequence of events is confirmed by the series
of medallions which frequently borders the large central tauroctonos
representations, such as the wall fresco in the Mithraeum at Marino
and the relief found at Virunum, to give only two examples.

In the Marino sequence, reading the right panel from top to bottom,
we find scenes of (1) Mithra dragging the captured bull to the cave, (2) Sol
kneeling before Mithra, (3) Sol and Mithra concluding a pact before an
altar, and (4) Mithra striking the rock from which the life-giving water
gushes. In the homage medallion, Mithra raises a mysterious object in the
air as if he is going to hit Sol, who kneels before him with outstretched hands.
Vermaseren has not explained this type of scene fully, especially in regard
to the mysterious object in Mithra's hand. He says that it looks like a piece of
meat—a shoulder or a leg—with which Mithra will hit Sol.[6] In the Marino
Mithraeum the object quite clearly seems to be a piece of meat. But
why a piece of meat? It seems likely that it is a part of the life-imparting
bull, which Mithra has just slain in the cave. It is symbolic of the new power
loosed by the dying lunar bull. But the scene under discussion occurs
after the bull-slaying. It may be significant also that in the pact scene, which
follows, a meat offering is shown on the altar between Sol and Mithra.
This could indicate the practice of offering up a choice part of the sacrificial
victim. It would thus be a foretaste of the banquet to follow immediately
after the pact of friendship.[7] Therefore, the concord between the gods was
not established until after the slaying of the bull. The slaying was a
signal act of obedience by Mithra at the command of Sol.

6. *Ve-Mi*, p. 96.
7. *Cu-Mi*, p. 132.

After this, Mithra assumes command, crowns Sol, makes peace with
him, dines with him, and finally ascends with him. The cycle which began
with the seven-rayed sun-god in heaven ends with the ascent of both
gods again. Celestial peace is brought about by the death of the bull and the
creation that ensues, and now the covenant of concord is represented in
the common meal. From the moment of the pact on, there is a unified deity
for the worshipers. Mithra is no longer a lesser divine being; he assumes
the authority and the titles of Sol. Henceforth he is known as *Deus
Sol Invictus.* He is often represented, like Sol, holding a blue orb, the symbol
of the kosmos over which he rules as kosmokrator.

Such a sequence of events helps to explain the relationship of Sol and
Mithra; that is, how one character can appear to be supreme in one scene and
another character in another scene. Cumont's sequence indicates that Mithra
is all-powerful at the beginning of his relations with Sol and subsequently
is commissioned to slay the bull. Our reconstruction of the myth eliminates
this contradiction, for Mithra becomes pre-eminent after the bull-slaying.[8]

If the foregoing order of the mythical events is correct, the liturgical
action based upon it would have been:

1. The sacrifice of an animal or bird recalling the bull-slaying by
   the representative of Mithra, the *Pater*.
2. A ritual subjection and coronation of the representative of Sol,
   the *Heliodromus* (Courier of the Sun) by the *Pater*, signifying the
   pre-eminence of Mithra.
3. A pact, perhaps made with the offering of a part of the sacrifice
   on the small altar, the *Pater* and *Heliodromus* playing the
   liturgical roles.
4. The cult meal, with the *Pater* and *Heliodromus* as chief *officiantes*,
   offering the participants a mystical foretaste of the soul's ascent
   with Sol and Mithra.

Here the liturgical unity is apparent. There are acts of preparation leading
up to the climactic meal. Here also is seen a basic principle in antique pagan

8. Cf. the Hymn of Humiliation-Exaltation in Phil. 2:6–11 and the Jewish charges
that the Christians were polytheists worshiping two gods.

religion: the acts of the mythology are liturgically imitated so that their saving efficacy may be realized by the worshiper. Such a unified main liturgy would explain the frequency of small scenes involving Sol and Mithra, for they would constitute integral parts of the liturgy along with the banquet as the culminating point of the ritual. It would further explain the function of the altar, or altars, which are always present in the sanctuaries as standard pieces of equipment for the ceremonies. The sacrifice and the distribution of the holy food commemorated the covenant between Mithra and Sol and offered eschatological hope of a union with them in the world beyond.

The nature of the Mithraic meal has already been well explained by Vermaseren. Bread, cake, meat (bull, cock, ram, or pig), grapes, and, less often, fish are seen in the various banquet scenes.[9] A *krater* (bowl) is seen again and again in Mithraic art. In several German reliefs it appears in the bull-slaying scene, located directly under the bull.[10] And in the Mithraeum under Santa Prisca in Rome, the bowl is carried in the processional scene on the left wall, along with the bread and tapers (?) as the attendants approach the feast of Mithra and Sol. Thus the krater would appear to hold blood or a symbolic substitute used in the meal—perhaps wine, as Vermaseren has suggested. It is likely that the krater often held water as a substitute for the bull's blood. In the Mithraeum of the Seven Doors at Ostia, for instance, the krater is portrayed in a monochrome mosaic as a symbol of the element water. Justin says that bread and water were used in the mysteries of Mithra.[11] Thus, water was used at the various cult meals as well as blood and wine. It is possible that this is the meaning of Proclus' reference to the *pegaios krater*, the life-giving (literally, the "springing-up") bowl, though he may have had in mind the various floor basins used for purificatory rites.

Although it is not possible to reconstruct every detail of the liturgical activity, it is possible that there was a ceremonial procession at the banquet celebration. In the Mithraeum under Santa Prisca the fresco on the left wall

9. *Ve-Mi*, pp. 101–3.
10. *Ve-Corp*, II, Figs. 274, 340, 347.
11. *Apol.* 1. 66.

depicts a procession of cult participants who are carrying various objects toward the seated figures of Sol and Mithra. It was perhaps in this procession that the participants made a symbolic passage through the seven planetary spheres of salvation. At Ostia the seven spheres are portrayed on the mosaic floor of the Mithraeum of the Seven Spheres and are symbolized again in the Mithraeum of the Seven Doors.[12] In the Mithraeum of Felicissimus the signs of the seven grades of initiation, which correspond to the seven planetary spheres, could represent the seven steps of salvation as one proceeded from the rear of the sanctuary to the front (Plates 21–28; see also Plate 3).[13]

When we turn to consider the participants in the mysteries of Mithra, we are again faced by a scarcity of evidence. Their activity was not confined to the central cult ceremony. There were various ceremonies of initiation into the cult and into the various grades. There are scraps of information available about various procedures in the initiation rituals, but it is difficult to form a full outline of each of the separate ceremonies from the fragmentary evidence at hand. Vermaseren believes that the *syndexi* ("initiates with the right hand") of the cult imitated the pact made by Mithra and Sol, who also joined right hands in brotherhood, according to Persian custom.[14] One can also find the mythical motif of submission to torturous trials repeated in the ordeals of the initiates. These could call to mind the trials of Mithra. Gregory of Nazianzus mentions the "tortures and burnings (or brandings)" of the Mithra cults.[15] And the frescoes of the Capua Mithraeum—the most complete pictorial representation of initiations—show the initiate at first standing, then kneeling and even prostrate, as he undergoes the ordeals of initiation. The investiture of Sol by Mithra may be reflected in the initiation into the grade of Soldier, if Tertullian accurately describes the initiate's rejection of a proffered crown by saying that Mithra's alone is his wreath and that his wreath rests in his god.[16]

---

12. Cf. Celsus' mention of the ladder of seven gates in *Contra Celsum* 6. 21.
13. *Ve-Mi*, pp. 157–58.
14. *Ibid.*, p. 137.
15. *Oratio* IV, *Contra Julianum* I. 52, *Hist. Aug. Comm.* 9.
16. *De corona* 15.

PLATE 21   Votive Inscription of Felicissimus (with the seven grades
in the following plates)

PLATE 22   The First Mithraic Grade: Corax, Mercury

PLATE 23　The Second Mithraic Grade: Nymphus, Venus

PLATE 24   The Third Mithraic Grade: Miles, Mars

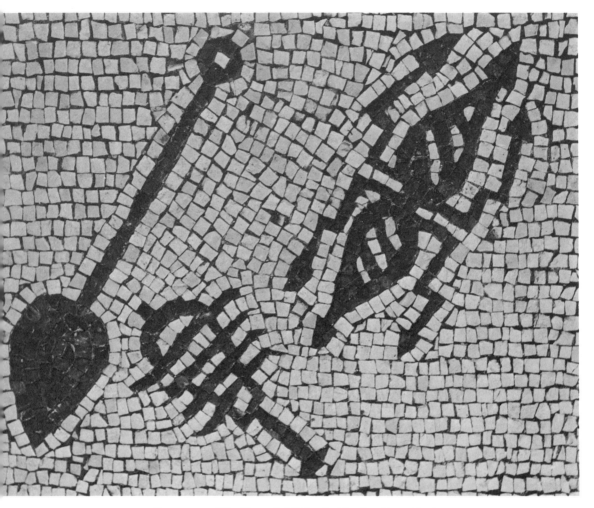

PLATE 25   The Fourth Mithraic Grade: Leo, Jupiter

PLATE 26 The Fifth Mithraic Grade: Perses, Luna

PLATE 27   The Sixth Mithraic Grade: Heliodromus, Sol

PLATE 28   The Seventh Mithraic Grade: Pater, Saturn

It would be illuminating if one were able to determine which of the
initiation ceremonies was a prerequisite to full participation in the
main liturgy. Was the first initiation into the cult the only necessary step
for full participation in the meal, or did one have to attain a higher
grade in order to have full privileges? The answer to this question
must be tentative. It is possible only to point to a few bits of evidence
that indicate various levels of participation by cult members.

The division of many sanctuaries indicates that there was a variety of
liturgical function within the seven grades. At Ostia one can observe several
ways in which the Mithraic sanctuaries are divided by wall structures,
floor decorations, and placement of the podium niches (see Plate 14). These
divisions may mean that the grades were arranged according to rank for the
liturgy. The lower grades would have remained at the back of the sanctuary.

The symbols of the seven grades in the floor of the Mithraeum
of Felicissimus are arranged from the lowest to the highest as one walks from
the back of the sanctuary to the front. The procession in the right wall
fresco of the Santa Prisca Mithraeum shows the seven grades arranged in
exactly the same order.[17] It seems safe to conclude from this evidence
that the lower grades sat at the back of the sanctuary and probably
had a subordinate role to play in the ceremony.

Porphyry gives us more exact information about the mode of participation
in the cult. According to him there were four grades of "participants" (the
higher grades), who took part fully in the meal, and three grades of
"attendants" (the lower grades), who acted as servants but did not partake
of the meal.[18] Vermaseren, however, postulates that the attendants
could have been participants and vice versa.[19]

In artistic portrayals of the meal scene, it is always Mithra and Sol
who partake of the meal together. In some scenes there are other persons
representing certain grades, but they are in most cases serving and not
reclining with the two gods. Examples of such scenes are: the reversible relief

17. Jerome *Ep.* CVII *Ad Laetam.*
18. Porphyry *De abstinentia* IV. 16.
19. *Ve-Mi*, p. 140.

from Heddernheim,[20] in which two youths in Oriental clothing stand next
to the two gods; a relief from Rückingen,[21] in which two servants are
present; and perhaps the best example, from Dalmatia,[22] in which
four attendants are pictured, one in a raven's mask, two in Phrygian caps,
and another in a lion's mask.[23] However, there is at least one exceptional case
in which three persons recline for the meal instead of two. This scene is
from Merida, Spain.[24] There are also three standing figures who are attendants.
A damaged panel of the fresco in the Palazzo Barberini Mithraeum in
Rome may represent three persons reclining for the feast.[25]

The mosaic floor of the Mithraeum of Lucretius Menander at Ostia
contains several small marble blocks laid out in a symmetrical pattern. In this
pattern five blocks lie in the back half of the sanctuary behind the marble
dividing strip and two lie directly in front of the altar. The five are distributed
so that three lie in a horizontal line near the entrance to the sanctuary
and two lie on either side of the floor directly before the dividing strip. These
blocks may have had some liturgical function, marking positions where
a representative of each grade stood during the ceremony. In this grouping the
five persons in the back of the room might have been of a different rank
from the two standing before the altar. This arrangement would be in accord
with the division in the meal scenes in which Sol and Mithra sit alone.

Could this mean that only the two top grades partook of the meal? Possibly;
but benches were provided as standard equipment for the whole sanctuary
and not just part of it (with the exception of the Mithraeum of the Animals).
This leads us to think that all participated in the meal itself in some way.
Yet they were attendants and as such had a much lower status than the Father
and the Courier of the Sun. They may not all have partaken in equal fashion
in the meal. It has been noted that there was a major division between

20. *Ve-Corp*, II, Inscr. 1083.
21. *Ibid.*, II, Inscr. 1137.
22. *Ibid.*, II, Inscr. 1896.
23. On the use of animal masks in the Mithraic ceremonies see Origen *Contra Celsum* VI. 33.
24. *Ve-Corp*, I, Inscr. 782, Fig. 214.
25. *Ibid.*, I, Inscr. 390.

the two highest grades and the five lowest. There may also have been a division of function and position among the five lower grades. In the Mithraeum of Lucretius Menander there are two groupings visible among the five liturgical positions; two are nearer to the altar, while three are farther back, toward the rear of the sanctuary. These groupings could have meaning for the degree of participation. It is our conclusion that all grades probably partook of the meal, but, since they did not share equally in the liturgy, they may not have shared equally in the meal.

The importance of studying the Mithraic liturgy consists not only in a better understanding of a major antique religion—the primary concern of this paper—but also in its influence on the Christian doctrine and practice of the Eucharist. The Church Fathers accused Mithraism of aping their Eucharistic worship. But Christianity did not influence Mithraism in a one-sided exchange. Its Eucharist was probably influenced also by the sacred meal of Mithra and other contemporary pagan cult meals. This does not mean that the Christians readily copied what they saw in the pagan cults. They polemicized against it. But as they strove to prove the superiority of their meal, they used the naturalistic language of their rivals. In his work *Liber de errore profanarum religionum*, Firmicus Maternus refers to the food in pagan cults as "poison" (18.1) which kills in contrast to the bread and cup of Christ, which give life and immortality. Firmicus makes the claim for the Christian Eucharist that pagans made for their meal. Thus he adopts a magical understanding of the Eucharist which was inspired in part by the cult meal of Mithraism and other mystery cults. This subject, which deserves new research in patristic scholarship, makes the study of Mithraic liturgy even more valuable.

Christ and Mithra

SAMUEL LAEUCHLI

W HAT IS THE RELATION between Christianity and the mystery religions, above all, between the worship of Christ and that of the Persian God?[1] Our studies at Ostia have demonstrated how essential and relevant this problem is and that it will demand new attention in the coming years. This is not the place to write a concluding statement, since any attempt to penetrate this vital issue, which is yet so intricate, would lead to a large monograph—a work we hope will be written in the near future not only because of the wealth of Mithraic discoveries in recent years but because of the urgency in this comparison for an understanding of ancient Christianity. Instead, we delineate certain tentative conclusions as they appeared to us at the end of our Ostia project.

1. The question is posed afresh by the Santa Prisca discovery; the Mithraeum stood beside a Christian sanctuary (*Ve-Prisc*, p. 114) until it was destroyed by the Christians (*Ve-Prisc*, pp. 241 ff.).

85

The Methodological Problem

In the heyday of the comparative history of religions, scholars were
intent on finding Mithraic parallels to Christian thought, art, and practice; in
the subsequent reaction, research sought primarily to establish the distinct
features in both religions. While the first tended to show the proximity
of the two religions, the second meant to prove their remoteness.[2]
But the problems are infinitely more complex. As a basic methodological
scheme, we reckon with a fourfold distinction:

a) A direct influence of Mithraism upon Christianity.
To anyone studying the material on Mithra, the possibility of
Mithraic influence appears in many instances.

b) A direct influence of Christianity on Mithraism. This is an option
which has not been taken seriously enough into consideration. We obviously
have Jewish influences on Gnosticism, Magna Mater influences on Mithraism,
Hellenistic religious influences on Judaism. In the whole context of
extreme syncretism as we find it in our period (Plate 29), influences have
frequently gone both ways, and there is no reason to assume that this should
not have been the case in the Christian impact on Mithraism.

c) A common root for Christian and Mithraic phenomena. Religious
elements can appear at two different places simply because they arose
from parallel origins. When you have the same element simultaneously, this
does not necessarily mean the priority of one over the other.

d) A common contemporaneousness resulting directly from this common
source. Two religions could have spoken to a Roman condition, a social
need, and a theological question without having learned from each other or
even without having known of each other's existence. As in so many other
instances of philosophy and literature, parallel thoughts and social patterns can
appear independently of one another as "new" elements with the authentic
consciousness of such newness. In any movement of a religion, the
context changes the content; if a religion moved into the Roman sphere,

2. *Ve-Corp*, I, 1–42; II, 1–7.

86

PLATE 29   The Good Shepherd (detail from a Christian sarcophagus)

the soil would have altered the content of different religions,
thereby creating striking parallels.

The more we delved into the Mithraic research at Ostia and compared
the data with early Christian phenomena, the more we realized that
the four alternatives must be constantly weighed against one another; that
choices are frequently impossible to make (because of the absence of so much
Mithraic material prior to the Hadrianic epoch); and that—worst of all—
more than one possible connection could be involved. Precisely because of the
fourth point above (point d), the first two are precarious; and yet cases
of dependence (the Christmas festival of the fourth century,
for instance) do certainly exist.

In addition, Mithraic research must be aware of the following:

a) Mithraism in the second century B.C. is not necessarily the same as
Mithraism in the third century A.D. In two hundred years a religion can
change radically—not its myth or its apparent lines of thought, but
its concrete place in the world, its real theological beliefs, and its social
structure. Metamorphosis exists not merely in explicit changes of
mythological language but in the subtle and hidden shifts behind a
seemingly unchangeable mythological façade.

b) Just as the Christianity of Numidia was essentially different from
Christianity in Alexandria, the Mithraic religion only appears to us as a unity
because we have the basic mythological language without the concrete
involvement and liturgies of the people who visited these Mithraea. Mithra's
function at Ostia may not have been Mithra's function at Dura Europos.

c) In research about Christianity and Mithraism we must distinguish
among conscious, explicit, and implicit contacts. That the Christians
were so little aware of the Mithraic brother is one of the baffling factors
in this field; yet it may really lead us to the heart of the matter
if we examine where conscious contacts (and thus conflicts) were
recognized and where they were ignored.

d) In determining parallels and distinctions, the analysis of this or that
word or symbol can be only part of the research. In the hermeneutic quest we
must also ask what impact was made by two similar or at least parallel

sanctuaries whose initiates may have represented but a small percentage of Ostia's populace. A comparison with Harnack's well-known estimate on the number of Christians in Rome is illuminating. If we reckon with 20 Mithraea (there may have been more), with a possible maximum figure of 50 in each sanctuary, conservatively counting, we would have to assume 1,000 believers at the zenith of Ostian Mithraism. Out of a possible 50,000 people in Ostia, they would thus comprise roughly 2 per cent. This is indeed not far from Harnack's 30,000 Christians in third-century Rome, who would represent approximately 3 per cent of a possible one million inhabitants.[5] Both figures are quite tentative, but they show that at Ostia we have to reckon with a Mithraic impact not too far removed from the relationship in Rome between the church and the pagan world. The infiltration of Mithra on such a scale into the Roman seaport, parallel to the eighty Mithraea in Rome itself,[6] serves as a symbol for the advent of new religious vitality from the East.[7]

The Ostia situation shows us the political and social aspects of this religious bankruptcy. Around the Forum we find the three impressive structures of imperial power: the Capitol, the temple to Roma and Augustus, and the Pantheon. In this triad appears the understructure of the empire that fought with the church. But the Mithraic house churches, private or semiprivate, were the new dynamic of second- and third-century Ostia, and they were no longer at the Decumanus but in the intimacy of houses. Here man found a social yet nonpolitical form of religious experience and identity. Whether this form was merely escape remains to be seen.

The influx of Mithra starts at a time when Rome was, externally speaking, still in a successful period, i.e., early in the Antonine age. This fact

5. Adolf von Harnack, *Die Mission und Ausbreitung des Christentums in den ersten drei Jahrhunderten* (Leipzig, 1924), II, 805. *Me*, pp. 532–34.

6. Mithraic material was found in practically every one of Rome's 14 regions, with the exception of Region 1 and perhaps 10 (*Ve-Corp*, pp. 327–519); in addition, there is a large amount of unplaceable material (*Ve-Corp*, pp. 520 ff. and 584 ff.).

7. This vitality did not reach the Roman aristocracy or even the ruling classes (*Me*, pp. 380 ff.). Yet it is amazing how many Latin and Latinized names are found in Mithraic inscriptions in the Western empire (cf. *Ve-Corp*, I, Inscrs. 356 ff.).

argues that the conditions for the great Roman disaster under Commodus existed much earlier. That Rome looked East for new religious vitality was not the result of external causes, such as the Marcomannian war or the economic disasters at the end of the century, but was the result of vast inner changes—philosophical, religious, and social—which had begun centuries before and which expressed themselves now in the victory of the East.

Two conclusions force themselves upon us. In the first place, Mithra in Ostia shows us the validity of speaking about the situation into which Christianity entered. The religious decay and the social readiness for a new cultic movement produced the soil on which the Eastern seed could fall, even though the flowering of that seed would depend precisely on the soil. The secret of the early Christian success was not success within a vacuum but within a particular historical situation. Against any docetic idealization of primitive Christianity, one must maintain the historicity of the Christian rise in the period between Trimalcho and Plotinus or between Tiberius and Commodus.

In this readiness of the empire to accept, not the ancient Roman mythology and what it symbolized, but the dynamic from the East, the question of the specific character of the Christian religion must be posed. From the material in Ostia one must ask indeed why Mithra lost and the church won so radically during the third and fourth centuries. To search for the authentic historical impact of Christian faith is not a demand of present-day apologetics alone; it is rather a demand of the historical situation itself. That Christianity defeated Mithra in one of antiquity's most fascinating religious contests must have had something to do not merely with Rome, and not merely with Mithra, but with Christianity's potential. We believe that here lie the elements of message and community, to which we shall turn later on.

The Mithraeum

The profound parallels between Christianity and Mithraism can be shown best in the Mithraic house church. As we have pointed out, here we find the transition from the ancient temple, with its external perfection, its bare cella, and its public symbol of sacrifice, to the inner cult room with its benches, its veiled symbolism, and its hidden ritual. Immediately we think of the *house church*, so essential to the understanding of early Christianity. In the Book of Acts we can trace the transition from public temple worship to the communal assembly in the houses of Jerusalem. As the church spread into the Mediterranean world, we can observe the movement from the temple to the synagogue and into the private house. The earliest archaeological evidence, the terminology, the literary texts, all speak of the vital place which the house church possessed in the rise of pre-Constantinian Christianity.[8] At the root of both Mithraeum and house church lay a transmutation of the temple religion for the sake of a new type of communal experience.

The problems of the origins of this duality and parallelism cannot be answered in our context, and all the methodological safeguards we have made at the outset must be considered. We do not know when and where that profound change, which probably goes back centuries before it appears in archaeological and textual evidence, began to occur. We must reckon with the synagogue and with the philosophical schools and religious sects of the Hellenistic age; we must also consider the Gnostic circles, the ramifications of the earliest mysteries, and the developments in Roman religion itself, such as funeral benches at Porto and the material in Petra. But we observe how the Christian house church developed in the fertile climate of a new religious expectation in the Roman world.

As a matter of fact, we can almost speak of a "gods are dead" problematic as basic to the impact made by Christianity and Mithraism on that world. The "religious"-political ideology of the Augustan imperium was dead before it was ever brought to daylight, and the gods of the Greeks and Romans obviously failed to speak. In the light of the Ostian Mithraea we understand the impact that the Christian community, with its agape feasts and home

8. Acts 2:46, 20:7–8. Cf. Willy Rordorf, "Was wissen wir über die christlichen Gottesdiensträume der vorkonstantinischen Zeit?" *Zeitschrift für neutestamentliche Wissenschaft*, LV (1964), 111 ff.

sanctuaries, must have made on a Roman looking for a new social identity and for fresh religious vitality. We understand that this impetus did not occur merely on an individualistic basis, namely, the individual quest for immortality and rebirth, but also on a communal one. The Mithraeum as well as the house church offered a corporate experience, no longer in the total framework of a state nor like that felt among the crowds at Eleusis; neither was it merely a personal initiation into eternal life. Birth came to man not merely in a new myth, or in a new historical reality, or both, but also in a certain bodily community within the enclosure of a new type of intimate sanctuary. This is precisely what Rome, without knowing it, needed so desperately. The temple became house, *aedes*.[9]

The Arcanum

In order to come to grips with the difference between Christ and Mithra, we must enter the issue of the "arcane" character of primitive Christianity (see Plates 30–32). It would demand total ignorance of texts to deny that by the fourth century Christianity had become an arcane religion. But when it comes to the first two hundred years of Christian history, scholars are divided on the arcane character of the Christian ritual, and a clear separation into arcane mystery and nonarcane Christianity has become for many an easy solution for a troublesome research problem.[10]

As we look at the archaeological material at Ostia, there comes into view a broad range of possibilities with regard to this problem. The Magna Mater temple, for example, is surely not fully arcane in its architecture, although its practice would certainly call for a mystery ritual.[11] In the Mithraea we find a clear attempt to get away from public life, for not

9. *Aedes: Ve-Corp*, I, Inscrs. 247, 433, 876; II, Inscr. 1968. *Templum: Be-Mi*, p. 26; *Ve-Corp*, I, Inscrs. 53, 228; II, Inscr. 842.

10. A. D. Nock, *Conversion* (London, 1933), pp. 204, 214; O. Perler, ("Arkandisziplin," *Reallexikon für Antike und Christentum*, I, 671 ff.) sees the arcane character in fourth-century Christianity but does not trace it back beyond Clem. Alex. *Protr.* 12 and Hipp. *Apost. Trad.* 16.

11. *Sq*, p. 5.

PLATE 30   The Phoenix as Symbol of Resurrection (floor mosaic
from the Baths of Neptune)

PLATE 31 "JESUS" Monogram (floor mosaic from the Baths of Neptune)

PLATE 32   Tree of Life; Fruit of Life (floor mosaic from the Baths of Neptune)

one is on a major thoroughfare; yet from the Imperial Palace to the underground sanctuary beneath the Baths of Mithra the *degree* of hiddenness certainly varies. These Mithraic churches, compared with cult niches, are not as radically arcane as one would expect them to be from reading research literature on secret religions. They belonged to city life but were hidden to a certain degree. They were *somewhat* accessible—the cave had become a room, and the remaining evidence often looks as if the cult was part of the living rhythm of at least the house in which it was found. The material makes us conclude that the problem cannot be posed in the traditional form of arcane or nonarcane religions.

Similar questions must be raised in regard to Christian texts. There is quite an emotional battle about Matt. 7:6—Jesus' word about not throwing pearls before swine. We find material during the patristic period, from the third to the fifth century, which can, at least, be interpreted as evidence for early arcane practices. The fact that such material is often twisted or ignored by research leads us to suspect that there is a Christian apologetic at work against any ties to the arcane practices of the mystery cults. Certain texts by the Church Fathers can be quoted against the arcane theory, and these are often early texts which speak of the open character of the Christian faith; yet, the way nonbelievers are dismissed before the Eucharist in the liturgy of the fourth century is an arcane practice. If not, then we must change the meaning of "arcane."[12] From the clearly arcane practices of the fourth century one cannot help looking back and asking: Does Matt. 7:6 have anything to do with *Didache?* Does *Didache* have anything to do with *Apost. Const.* 7.25?

It is the artificial limitation of the word "arcane" which must be challenged. Instead of a simple dichotomy between mystery ritual and nonarcane faith, there are different "arcane" dimensions.

a) *Arcane social exclusiveness.* A group closes itself off from the outside by some form of discipline. Qumran gives clear evidence for this.

---

12. *Did.* 9.5; Just. *Apol.* 1.61; Athan. *Apol. Sec.* 44.4; Hans Lietzmann, *From Constantine to Julian* (London, 1950), p. 291; *Apost. Const.* 8.6.

This social arcaneness could have political overtones; it could mean the formation of bodies within the state with powerful religious and social identities. Matt. 7:6, for instance, could indeed be void of all ritualistic meaning. If it were, its implications would create a broad and obvious distinction between this group and whoever are meant by the swine. When a group shuts itself off by some barrier, it does not thereby become a mystery cult in the historical sense, of course; but it forms a religious and social exclusiveness which, when broken off from its natural contexts, leads to the mysteries and is therefore related to ritualistic arcaneness.[13]

We observe here that there was nowhere—perhaps with the exception of a few Manichaean extremists—any *totally* arcane society. Even the Faustus of Augustine's age belonged to North African culture. The arcane dimensions are always modified. Unless the mystery cult fled from the world for good (which it never did!), its arcane character was always, on a social level, a compromise.

b) *Arcane theology.* Again, this phenomenon has been neatly separated from the ritual, and an attempt has been made to distinguish between the message and the cult. But there was, throughout Gnostic and early Christian theology, a strong element of the mystery, the revealed truth hidden to the world, the word given to those who are called to hear it. From the eschatological parable in the New Testament to Gregory of Nazianzus' saying that not everyone has a right to talk about theology, arcane theological dimensions are found throughout Christian and semi-Christian texts.[14] A theology of revelation creates a temenos of faith which is not open to the whole world. Again, the *mysterium* of the message is usually separated from the cult; but just as the hidden message belongs to a group which preaches this hiddenness, so it belongs to a group which practices it through some form or another.

c) *Arcane ritual.* Properly speaking, the mystery cults are defined by the arcane ritual; but that ritual took place within an exclusive community,

13. *Isaeus* 8. 17–18; Qumran, *Man. Disc.* 1.
14. Matt. 13:13; Greg. Naz. *Or.* 27. 5; *Evang. Ver.* 16. 31–33.

and it presented some form of teaching. Just as the first two elements (social exclusiveness and arcane theology) are obviously present in the church, soon arcane ritualistic practices are found. After all, *Didache* 9. 5 *does* talk about Matt. 7:6 in relation to the Eucharist! The texts on the secrecy of the Eucharist are not to be dismissed, and the ritual of Hippolytus, which contained a whole pageantry of exorcism, milk, honey, and robes, belongs to catechetical instructions.[15] The question, therefore, is surely not whether we can pin down a mystery cult to this third definition and free the early patristic church from it but rather *which* arcane elements are stronger in *which* religion and at *which* period.

All three dimensions are representative of the closing years of antiquity. All three contain a new religious-psychological search for security and return; they demonstrate the craving of ancient man for a safe, exclusive society; they present the many aspects in which theological truth was communicated through revealed, unheard-of channels; and they show the ritual through which initiation was possible. These elements were present in many religious and even nonreligious groups of this period (as the initiation into the Roman Senate indicates!).[16] If we decide to define the mystery cults as those which centered around ritualistic arcaneness, we must be aware that this hidden cultic nature belongs to a much wider framework in which religious movements resorted to different forms of thought, community, or cult— forms by which they could demonstrate a certain break with the world. From this we must conclude that gnosis, Qumran, the mystery cult, and the Christian church are related in their secrecy, a secrecy which began with social and theological exclusiveness and led to the hidden ritual, to the secrecy which—as the Mithraea of Ostia show—could under such circumstances never be called consistent or ultimate but which was, in its social, theological, or ritualistic aspects, at best one of degree.

Having viewed these points of contact between the Christian and Mithraic religions, we turn to the difference between them. One can ask

15. Hipp. *Apost. Trad.* 20.
16. Origen *Contra Celsum* 6. 11.

why Mithra lost and Christ won. Or one can pose the question another way: Was there an essential difference which would account for the diverse direction these related cults took? We shall talk first about the message and then about the community.

The Message

The Christian church preserved a body of writings which contained a cogent message. In these documents are eschatological parables, historical writings, letters, and an apocalyptic vision. The life of the early church is intricately tied in with this message; yet the message stands in a strange contrast to the ritual of salvation, to the sequence of Christian life, and even to patristic theology and Christology. Between the message and its history there exists a painful discordance.

We come to grips with this discordance as soon as we compare the Biblical message with the Mithraic one. It would indeed be a grave error to neglect the "message character" of the Mithraic ritual. Here was a *kerygma*, the message of death and new life, of conquest through individual and communal discipline, of gradual ascent toward Sol.[17] The mystery cult had a set of phrases, ethically and psychologically relevant, speaking directly to the need of the time. And it was a simple message, a clear path toward life and immortality.

In contrast to Mithra, the Christian gospel did not have a uniform message. Its parables are veiled; its eschatology was disturbing. The paradoxical ethic of the Synoptics was not what the Roman psyche either wanted or needed. Arising from obvious tensions among the different books, the Christian message virtually demanded theological conflict, as the early church soon found out. The letters of Paul were difficult reading even to the early Christians, who understood them only partially. While the cult ritual of the mystery was as lucid as it could be, the Christian message

17. Lines 12–17 of the Santa Prisca inscriptions give an excellent example (*Ve-Prisc*, pp. 211 ff.).

was not linear but disturbingly pluralistic, creating problems
in Christology, in liturgy, and in discipline.

To be sure, Mithra had problems. If Mithraic theologians had been
at work, a Nicaean battle could have arisen over the duality of Sol and Mithra.
But in Mithraism such a point of conflict does not seem to have been reached,
because, where the message is subservient to the cult, one can ignore theology.
The essential difference is that Christianity had a message which stood
over against all the cultic and social forms of church life, just as original
Christian texts stood over against the theological positions of the church. The
Johannine literature was a preface to the Gnostic battle; the texts on
temptation and the Cross helped produce the Nestorian controversy; the
Arian fight was nothing but a commentary on the New Testament. Here
were historical texts, centering around a historical person, containing foreign
elements that refused to fit the pattern of the church in the second and
third centuries. Between the texts and their "translations" there
lurked dangerous conflicts, as are exhibited in Montanism, Origen, Tertullian;
or Antony, Julian of Ecclanum, Theodore of Mopsuestia.

We could point to the amazing tension in Christianity between the
individual and the eschatological. Primitive Christian texts were apocalyptic,
using patterns of late Jewish culture; but at the same time they forced the
individual into a threatening and yet very fertile eschatological tension, a front
against the world. Christianity soon gave up its primitive apocalypticism
as an essential part of its faith; but the eschatological concern returned in a
different context to create the salt of patristic history from Montanus to
Benedict. Eschatology meant not merely hope of immortality but suspension
of time and *kosmos*. Even in its obvious demythologizations (which had to
set in as soon as the texts were written down!) its poetry remained a hidden
as well as potentially explosive force behind the life of the church.

Theologians speak a great deal about "meeting the needs of the times."
Christianity did meet those needs, and the Christian ritual was adapted to the
atmosphere of mystery for which ancient man longed (Plate 33); and, as
in Mithra and Isis, this ritual was accompanied by strict ethical requirements.
But the strength of Christianity—over against Mithra and Isis—lay in the

PLATE 33   Chalice with the Fish (Christian floor mosaic from the
House of the Fishes)

opposite direction. In regard to the needs of the time, the *message* did *not* fit; eschatology disturbed the individual (even to the degree of driving him into absurd asceticism); the veiled message was not a simple unity. The power of Christianity lay in texts, theological as well as poetic, which claimed a life of their own and which thereby created the drama of Christian history. Mithra had history, but it had no theological and communal drama which tore this history apart.[18]

The Community

The second factor behind the Christian victory is the community. We have already noted the importance of the social dimension for an understanding of Mithraism in the Roman empire. We believe that it is this same social phenomenon which broke Mithra in favor of the Christian church. In both the Mithraic and the Christian material we are impressed by the world-wide impact, stretching from the Libyan Desert to Hadrian's Wall; and in both we detect the offer of a new communal experience where other mystery cults offered merely individualistic rebirth. Mithra had a *Pater Patrum*, like the bishop of a major Roman city, and his community in Ostia reached into a rather well-to-do villa called the Imperial Palace.[19]

But now comes the crucial distinction. From its Hebraic origins, the Christian community inherited a strong external, even political, function, a trait which was easily and dangerously well adapted to the Roman understanding of law and public religion. Beginning with Ignatius, the office of the Christian bishop assumed a style that cannot hide political undertones. We detect a desire in patristic history to break the Christian community open, to counteract mystery trends in its midst; why else would Justin Martyr emphasize that Christianity was *not* hidden?[20] Between the

18. One cannot verify the absence of frictions, of course. But there is no trace of any in the pagan or Christian material (Plut. *De Isid. et Osir.* 46; Porph. *De abst.* 2. 25 and 4. 16; Origen, *Contra Celsum* 6. 21, etc.).

19. *Ve-Corp*, I, Inscr. 336; cf. *Ve-Prisc*, pp. 178–80, and *Ve-Corp*, I, Inscr. 352.

20. Ign. *Eph.* 3. 2; Just. *Apol.* 1. 61.

mystery character of Christian communities and a public thrust within these communities there was a sharp discrepancy. While the mystery became more and more arcane, the church became political.

The decision between Christianity and Mithraism must have been reached in the third century. The archaeological and textual material shows us that Mithraism lost out in the time of the later soldier-emperors; Aurelian did not choose Mithra but the Syriac Sol Invictus.[21] It was during this century that we find the Christian church growing into a powerful body, and it was during the soldiers' rule that this powerful body was attacked systematically, for the first time under Decius. Partly because of the amalgamation of Hebraic and Roman notions, and partly because of the original Jewish kernel in the midst of that amalgamation, the Christian church responded to a public challenge as it refused to perform the sacrifice to the imperial idols. Mithra had no conflict with the empire.

Theologically this case receives interesting support. Despite its communal attraction, the Mithraic experience was still mainly vertical, directed toward the sun and toward individual immortality, found in the community of initiates. Through its conflict with the empire, the Christian faith received a political, vitally horizontal dimension. Faith, said Basil of Caesarea, was unthinkable in its first command (the love of God) without the second (the love of the brother).[22] Theologically, salvation and redemption were not merely individualistic experiences within the community but they were part of the life of this community, as forgiveness, penance, and the Eucharistic banquet. While Mithra remained an arcane religion, Christian theology forced the church into becoming a horizontal body to a degree which created the precarious Constantinian church. The forces which won out over Mithra won in the Nicaean church!

One item in the daily life of the communities illuminates the difference. With possible exceptions, the worshipers of the Sol Invictus were male believers, just as they always had been.[23] How can you turn the cult

21. Flav. Vopisc. *Aur.* 25. 4–6 and 35. 3; cf. *Cu-Mi*, pp. 185–86.
22. Bas. *Reg. Fus. Tract.* 7.
23. *Ve-Corp*, I, Inscr. 115; Porph. *De abst.* 4. 16.

within a spelaeum into the cult within a home, or a semipublic office, without letting the whole family, particularly the wives, partake in it? To be sure, Christianity in antiquity did not successfully rid itself of its ancient cultural fetters, for it still accorded "second-class citizenship" to its women; nevertheless, the presence of women in the church, a heritage from the synagogue community, shows how the earthly community was taken much more seriously in Christianity than in Mithra.

Finally, we can show the communal, terrestrial hardiness of the church in one last example. The Hebraic communality of the early church was not actually fully realized; the Christian church was one only in its hope and in some of its political arrogance. It is the disunity of the church which marks the contrast against, and the strength over, Mithra. The Christian church's disunity revealed the desperate struggle for concrete communality, for a body which takes seriously—in both Hebrew and Roman traditions—the earthly character of community.

From the Ostian Mithraea we can learn, indirectly, a great deal about the force of early Christianity. The church could identify with the empire; it became Roman, assuming thought patterns of the secular world and cult forms of the mysteries. But, in its second step, Christianity turned against the Roman world. The history of the early Christian church is a fascinating movement from message to translation and back to the message; or, from the origins to relevance to the criticism of relevance. Such is the dual movement of patristic Christianity. Christian eschatology was never given up entirely; there remained—despite any demythologization of its original apocalyptic imagery—the tension between history and myth, between myth and translation, and between translation and the original message.

Glossary

aedes	A Roman house
aedicula	A narrow, tall, free-standing structure of masonry and brick, sometimes rounded on top, in which is often found an elevated niche for representations of gods
arcanum	"Arcane," pertaining to a secret or mysteriously hidden dimension of cult, society, architecture
Bellona	The Latin goddess of war
bema	A structure of brick and mortar rising by steps or stages to an elevated platform
Bona Dea	Roman goddess whose arcane cult was strictly reserved for women
caseggiato	A large complex of apartments and shops, larger than an *insula*
cella	The inner sanctuary of a temple

Chryphius	The second grade of Mithraic initiation
collegiate temple	A shrine of a guild or trade association
Corax	The Raven; first grade of Mithraic initiation
Decumanus	An east-west street in a Roman city or camp; *Decumanus maximus:* the main east-west street in Ostia Antica
dendrophori	Participants in the Magna Mater procession who carried the sacred tree
domus	A Roman house, usually a single-family residence
falx	The Sichel, used as fertility symbol in Mithraic mosaics
gnosis	The revealed knowledge in Gnostic and early Christian thought
Gnosticism	A philosophical-religious movement of the second century
Heliodromus	The sixth grade of Mithraic initiation
horrea	Warehouse
immolation	Sacrificial killing of an animal (*immolatio boum:* of bulls)
insula	A large building or block, divided into many apartments
kerygma	The early Christian message
krater	A bowl
lararium	The sanctuary to the Lares in a Roman house
Leo	The Lion; fourth grade in Mithraic initiation
Magna Mater	Great Mother; fertility cult from Phrygia
mensa	Table; replacing the altar in Christian as well as certain Mithraic sanctuaries

Miles	The Soldier; third grade of Mithraic initiation
Mithraeum	The sanctuary in which Mithra was worshiped
nymphaeum	An ornamental fountain the components of which are usually a tank or basin with columns and statues and sometimes niches
Pater	The seventh and highest grade of Mithraic initiation
Perses	The fifth grade of Mithraic initiation
podium	A sloping bench or banquette of brick and mortar on which the Romans reclined
sistrum	The ritual rattle used in the worship of Isis
Sol Invictus	The "invincible sun"; a designation of the sun-god
spelaeum	A cave; symbolic sanctuary of Mithraism
taurobolium	The rite in which a bull is slain and its flowing blood pours over the initiate in a kind of baptism
tauroboliati	Those who have received the blood bath (in the Magna Mater cult)
tauroctonos	The stylized relief of Mithra slaying the primeval bull by pulling back its head and plunging a knife into its throat
temenos	The sacred ground around a temple or sanctuary

List of Plates

Index